Walking Down the Stairs

Poets on Poetry

Donald Hall, General Editor

Walking Down the Stairs

Selections from Interviews

GALWAY KINNELL

Ann Arbor   The University of Michigan Press

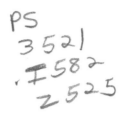

Library of Congress Cataloging in Publication Data

Kinnell, Galway, 1927-
Walking down the stairs.

(Poets on poetry)
1. Kinnell, Galway, 1927-   —Interviews.
2. Poetry.   I. Title.   II. Series.
PS3521.I582Z525   811'.5'4   77-23752

Grateful acknowledgment is made to the following authors, publishers, and journals for permission to reprint adaptations, excerpts, and selections from copyrighted material:

Anyart Journal for "An Interview with Ken McCullough," *Anyart Journal* 2, no. 6 (March 1977).

Brockport Writers Forum for "An Interview with A. Poulin, Jr., and Stan Sanvel Rubin," edited from a prose transcription of a videotape interview with Galway Kinnell in November, 1971, sponsored by the Brockport Writers Forum, Department of English, State University College, Brockport, N.Y. 14420. All rights reserved, State University of New York.

To Marion Magid

Preface

When I sat down at my desk heaped up with interviews of myself, to see if I could fulfill a long-postponed agreement to try to collect them into a book, I felt quite glum about the project. I don't like to read reviews of my work; worse by far was the prospect of working my way through this pile of ruminations. Moreoever, the topmost interview, dated 1966, began on a distinctly unpromising note: "Mr. Kinnell, I've never read any of your poetry, but I'd like to ask you a few questions about it. . . ."

I had submitted to these interviews willingly, of course. No doubt I was flattered by the presumption that my opinions could be worth publishing. But in my memories of being interviewed, I too often saw myself casting about for something—anything—that would get me past one question, on to the next, and so one step closer to the end. I saw myself often times bridling at perfectly reasonable questions. I am not the ideal subject. As I sat down to confront these conversations, I guessed I would savor the full meaning of the phrase, *to eat one's words.*

My forebodings proved accurate. Many foolish words had indeed been spoken. I was also impressed by my inability to speak in complete sentences. I seemed naturally to prefer the meandering kind of syntax that Eisenhower had improvised in order to bemuse reporters at his press conferences—a syntax at which I had often laughed pityingly. As I read, I ate many words, and the laughter as well.

But the uncanny aspect of the experience of reading this talk was that, in spite of all that was embarrassing, I found myself moderately beguiled by much of what I had to say, and intrigued by a number of forgotten remarks that I would not have recognized as my own, had they not been captured and given back by the tape recorder.

As I proceeded I noticed that the same questions kept recurring in the various interviews. At first it seemed to me that all this repetition was a weakness. I felt I would have to correct it or abandon the project. But as I read further, I began to see that the interviewers asked the same basic questions not because they all think alike, and not because I offer an especially narrow target, but because these are the natural and interesting questions. The repetition of them gives the book a certain unity, and all my fragmentary replies add up to statements that have a certain completeness. This was the surprising thing for me—to see that behind my own back, so to speak, I had evolved in these conversations a somewhat coherent set of ideas about poetry.

Some of the questions, of course, don't have anything to do with ideas. They ask only for personal testimony: Have I always wanted to be a poet? How did I begin writing? How do I start a poem? Do I revise? What do I do about dry spells? Do I find translating useful? Which poets do I read? And so on. This class of questions could be labeled gossip, albeit of a high order.

Frequently the interviewers ask for exegesis of certain poems. It is a modern assumption that there is a key to every poem and the author has it. The trouble is that I don't believe this. I happen to think that the author may be the last one to know what his work is about. I've often noticed that the more I like a poem I've written, the less sure I am that I can explicate it. I doubt if things have changed much since Socrates interviewed the poets of Athens, who proved quite unable to say what their poems were about. While an author can clear up certain small confusions, in general he is too involved in what he wanted the poem to be, to be able to see what it actually is. A number of times in these interviews I try to explain my poems. Reading through these efforts, I observed that my answers have mostly to do with circumstances and thoughts at the time of writing. In this way, I'm afraid, I drive the interviews back to the level of gossip again.

There are also questions that have to do with poetry in its technical aspects—questions about formal poetry, free verse, the music of the poem, its voice or persona, the role of autobiography, about symbols, metaphors, narrative, about the differences between fiction and poetry and between the long and short poem, and about language itself. I have always firmly believed that in poetry there is no such thing as technique that can be talked about apart from the poems that use it. Several times during the interviews, in fact, I express this opinion. Therefore I was quite surprised to see how cheerfully I held forth about these very matters. Apparently the interview is good occasion for dragging from a reluctant subject opinions he doesn't think he holds.

Then there are the "big" questions: How do you teach poetry? Why do you give poetry readings? Is there any point to political poetry? What is the use of poetry in a technological civilization? What is the relation of modern poetry to tribal poetry? These seem to reflect a curiosity about what it is like to be a poet in America today, and beyond that, what poetry is and what its purposes are—and a worry that poetry may be an anachronism, fated soon to die out. If my answers to these large questions are not very complete, I hope they at least convey something of my unsettled and changing feelings, my despair and my hope.

Honest men differ on how far you can go in changing the transcript of an interview for publication. Some people regard the actual spoken interview as a preliminary device to indicate the topics that are to be covered by the published document. They then write out the "interview" from scratch and revise and polish it as carefully as if it were an essay. For the purists, at the other extreme, spontaneity is everything—though even they allow that you may (1) make yourself speak in complete sentences and (2) cut where necessary to avoid making a total ass of yourself.

While a single interview should keep fairly close to the original conversation—the way you respond to questions tells something about you that can't be communicated in any other way—an entire book of interviews is another matter. Unless you can be spontaneous *and* articulate—which I can't—a little spontaneity goes a long way. I do think it's necessary that the answers be fairly thoughtful and coherent if a book of this kind is to be at all readable.

Therefore, I have revised the interviews, in the following ways. I tried to take out the more embarrassing passages—many huge chunks and countless small bits—whatever was notably dull, rambling, self-involved, self-serving, falsely modest, or otherwise unpleasant. (I know this is a dangerous admission.) Also, I changed the wording of many phrases. I expanded many half-articulated thoughts. I entirely rewrote many perfunctory or muddled answers. A few times when I rewrote answers I found they no longer would fit back into their original places. These I put into the interview with Don Bredes and David Brooks, an interview which is partly based on actual conversations, partly a repository of fragments from other interviews, and partly a literary composition. But enough of this. Anyone who might be curious can look up an original interview: a number of them have appeared in magazines and one took place on videotape.

In many ways it would have been better if another person had edited this book. Editing one's own conversations is, to say the least, an odd activity. It made me think of the cow on her hillside, swallowing and re-swallowing a meal already tasting too much of herself. The true reason I chose to edit the book myself is the phenomenon known as *l'esprit de l'escalier*: the remarks you think of as you walk down the stairs at the end of a dinner party, that would have made you the toast of Paris if only you'd thought of them a bit sooner. In this book I have had the one chance I'm likely ever to have to go back and try again. I did not find it possible to resist.

The title, *Walking Down the Stairs*, is a misnomer, of course, for the book consists not so much of after-thoughts of as actual conversations that have been more or less "improved." But out of respect for the honor system governing published interviews, according to which one should sound as one really sounds, I wanted a title that would confess at once to the violations of the code that turns parts of this book into fiction.

Perhaps I need not have worried. When I finished going through this collection of my own words—adding some, leaving some, changing some, eating some, ruminating them all—I could see that the whole thing is already fiction. The central character—that poet who has such an impressive *œuvre* behind him; who advises young writers; who successfully teaches them how to write poetry; who is petitioned by them, not without a certain bitterness, to read and pronounce on their manuscripts; who is reviewed and praised and reviled; who gets interviewed and pontificates at the least urging (often on subjects he knows nothing about) and goes so far as to publish a book of interviews of himself—that grand literary personage, alas, isn't me at all. The conventions of the interview form exist for the purpose of establishing the importance, or if that's not possible, the self-importance, of the subject. My impression is that the important self-important poet who holds forth in the pages to come is a creation of the *genre*. In reality, I feel about myself in the completely ordinary way I've always felt, since before I ever published a poem.

It has been interesting for me to read and work over these interviews. Now I'm tired of them. I'm tired—as the diligent reader soon will be—of hearing the one impersonating Kinnell going on at length about the one he thinks is Kinnell. Now I step out of the fiction that rules these pages, go to a freshly cleared desk, and sit down to write poetry again, a form of expression in which there is at least the possibility of finding oneself as one is.

Galway Kinnell
New York City
November 29, 1976

Contents

I

An Interview with
William Heyen and Gregory Fitz Gerald

Brockport, New York, October 1969

Fitz Gerald: You have written a number of poems about warfare. I'm thinking especially of the "Vapor Trail" poem.

Vapor Trail Reflected in the Frog Pond

1

The old watch: their
thick eyes
puff and foreclose by the moon. The young, heads
trailed by the beginnings of necks,
shiver,
in the guarantee they shall be bodies.

In the frog pond
the vapor trail of a SAC bomber creeps,

I hear its drone, drifting, high up
in immaculate ozone.

2

And I hear,
coming over the hills, America singing,
her varied carols I hear:
crack of deputies' rifles practising their aim

on stray dogs at night,
sput of cattleprod,
TV groaning at the smells of the human body,
curses of the soldier as he poisons, burns, grinds, and stabs
the rice of the world,
with open mouth, crying strong, hysterical curses.

3

And by rice paddies in Asia
bones
wearing a few shadows
walk down a dirt road, smashed
bloodsuckers on their heel, knowing
the flesh a man throws down in the sunshine
dogs shall eat
and the flesh that is upthrown in the air
shall be seized by birds,
shoulder blades smooth, unmarked by old feather-holes,
hands rivered
by blue, erratic wanderings of the blood,
eyes crinkled up
as they gaze up at the drifting sun that gives us our lives,
seed dazzled over the footbattered blaze of the earth.

Heyen: That's a powerful poem. Would you tell us what's behind it, where it came from?

Kinnell: I wrote it during the early stages of the American involvement in the Vietnam war. Just off the dirt road that leads up to my house there's a frog pond. I used to walk down to the main road to get my mail, about a mile, then back to this pond, where I'd sit on the bank and read my letters. Often, I'd take a bath in the pond before going up home. One very beautiful day I was walking back up from the frog pond, naked, holding my clothes in one hand, my mail in the other. I could feel the sun sending its heat down on me and the heat radiating up from the earth. I felt come over me pure happiness. I felt totally alive and totally existing in my body. Then I looked up and saw the vapor trail of a Strategic Air Command bomber, a terrible defilement. I had recently come up from the South, a land then full of violence. Vermont had been for me a retreat from the rest of America; that day I felt its sanctuary was destroyed. The second part is a parody of Whitman's "I Hear America Singing," and the third an attempt to imagine how it might be for a Vietnamese person to be walking along a road in his own country, just before the American bombers appeared in his sky.

Heyen: The complaint is always made that these poems become polemical and therefore are fleeting and evanescent.

Kinnell: It is true, of course, that some poems separate humanity into two camps: We, the "good people," poets and lovers; and they, Rusk and Johnson, Nixon, and so on, the killers, who belong to a different species. But we are all related—as Etheridge Knight says in one of his poems, "I am all of them, they are all of me." The best poems about this war, as about other wars, have been those whose outrage does not cause the author to forget that he and his enemy are brothers. Whitman's war poems are like that; so are Wilfred Owen's. In Owen's last poem he imagines he meets in hell the man he has just killed—a "strange meeting" of accomplices. At the end of the *Iliad*, when Priam comes across the lines to visit Achilles, the two enemies reach an almost loving understanding, even though it is Achilles who has killed Priam's sons.

Heyen: I'd like to ask you about your poem, "How Many Nights." For me the critical point in this poem is the intrusive speech of the crow, whether it is an ironic, mocking sound, or something entirely different.

How many nights
have I lain in terror,
O Creator Spirit, Maker of night and day,

only to walk out
the next morning over the frozen world
hearing under the creaking of snow
faint, peaceful breaths . . .
snake,
bear, earthworm, ant . . .

and above me
a wild crow crying '*yaw yaw yaw*'
from a branch nothing cried from ever in my life.

Kinnell: I know the line about that crow is puzzling. In fact, when the poem was first published, some friends telephoned me, to ask whether I'd thought of the crow as benign or as an unwelcome presence. I wrote this bit of verse to explicate those last lines. It's called "The Mind."

Suppose it's true
that from the beginning, a bird has been perched
in the silence of each branch.

It is this to have lived—
that when night comes, every one of them
will have sung, or be singing.

I was thinking of those diagrams—I still don't know if they are of the nervous system or of the blood vessels—that show the brain in the shape of a tree. At moments of full consciousness all the birds would be singing. Whether or not the crow's cry is beautiful mattered less to me than that this hitherto mute region comes into consciousness. But it's true, the crow has associations that are different for each person, and there could be a very different reading of this poem.

Fitz Gerald: Your use of animal images in "How Many Nights" seems characteristic of many other poems in *Body Rags*. If I were to suggest that from the use of animal imagery you develop a kind of mythology, would I be reading too much into the poem?

Kinnell: Yes, there are many animals in my poems. I've wanted to see them in themselves and also to see their closeness to us. I don't think I've succeeded in creating a mythology in my poetry, but I know it's the dream of every poem to be a myth.

Fitz Gerald: In "The Bear" you mention this terribly powerful odor of the bear as if it had a kind of emotional intensity for you. What was it that led you to emphasize this aspect?

Kinnell: I've been close to bears but not close enough to smell them. So it has nothing to do with the actual smell.

Fitz Gerald: An act of the imagination, then?

Kinnell: Yes. An imaginary smell. Not descriptive or naturalistic, but having to do with our sympathetic feelings, our capacity to know the life of another creature by imagining it.

Fitz Gerald: Is there an essential difference between the kind of writing activity going into a novel and that going into a poem?

Kinnell: There is at least one important difference.

When writing a novel, your time has to be your own for a long period. You can't write a paragraph and wait a week before writing the next. Also, for me, writing a novel means conceiving of a world outside of myself, one populated with other beings, who are in relationship with each other. In a poem it is mostly an inner world. Perhaps it's the same ultimately, but at least while writing one looks in different directions.

Fitz Gerald: The poem then is the exploration of the inner self—here again the poet is metaphor for humanity, perhaps?

Kinnell: Probably. Often a poem at least starts out being about oneself, about one's experiences, a fragment of autobiography. But then, if it's really a poem, it goes deeper than personality. It takes on that strange voice, intensely personal yet common to everyone, in which all rituals are spoken. A poem expresses one's most private feelings; and these turn out to be the feelings of everyone else as well. The separate egos vanish. The poem becomes simply the voice of a creature on earth speaking.

Fitz Gerald: The poem is essentially outer directed, then, although it begins inside?

Kinnell: Yes, in the same sense that when you go deep enough within yourself, deeper than the level of "personality," you are suddenly outside yourself, everywhere.

Selections made by Galway Kinnell from a prose transcription of a videotape interview in October, 1969, sponsored by the Brockport Writers Forum, Department of English, State University College, Brockport, N.Y. 14420. All rights reserved, State University of New York.

II

An Interview with
Albert Goldbarth and Virginia Gilbert

Goldbarth: Quite a few years ago, Glauco Cambon, in *Recent American Poetry*, called "Easter" your best poem to date and took great relish in explicating the formal structure and obvious symbolism, and then he said you must "beware the dangers of the Dionysian imagination." I'm not sure what he means by "Dionysian," but in your own understanding of that term, would you say you've heeded his advice?

Kinnell: I've tried not to, if I understand what he means. Another reviewer warned me against what he called my concupiscent vocabulary. I've tried not to heed that advice either. How wonderful it would be to have a Dionysian imagination expressed in a concupiscent vocabulary!

Goldbarth: Why don't you give me your reactions to this quotation: "He seems to me a natural poet, humanly likeable, gentle, ruminative, but he is dishearteningly prolix. Prolixity is, of course, the foremost and perhaps only natural enemy of the natural poet. Mr. Kinnell is going to have to do battle with it. Some of these pieces are almost too trivial to be believed and even the best of them keep blurring into each other since there is no real division, nothing to individualize them. Poetry can do better than this, and so can Kinnell."

Kinnell: That's James Dickey, right? The book he's reviewing, *What a Kingdom It Was*, collects poems written over a ten-year period. It does contain some rather trivial poems—but to me this argues a meager production rather than prolixity. Some of the poems do run on too long. I don't think they are as blurred as he finds them. His was one of the first reviews I'd ever received; on the whole it pleased me.

Goldbarth: Is there work by anybody you particularly admire that you want to call experimental?

Kinnell: Not really. While many of the poets I most admire have written things that are different from anything that had been written before, they didn't often engage in that deliberate technical innovation I think of when I use the term "experimental." I imagine that in the *Duino Elegies*, for instance, Rilke wanted to write out truthfully all that he understood, and the last thing that concerned him was technical innovation. Whatever is innovative in Rilke's poetry follows rather than leads. Formally, Thoreau was doing something extremely old-fashioned—just keeping, and piecing together, a journal of his nights and days in the woods. I don't think "experimental" is the right word for original, unprecedented works like these, or like "Howl," or "Jubilate Agno," or "Song of Myself," or "The Marriage of Heaven and Hell."

Goldbarth: Did you serve an apprenticeship under any other poet?

Kinnell: When I was at Princeton, there were writing courses given by R. P. Blackmur and John Berryman. I didn't take them. I felt a certain scorn that there could be a *course* in writing poetry. It seemed contrary to the nature of the enterprise. Also, I think I was afraid Berryman and Blackmur wouldn't like my poetry. Looking back I think I was probably right.

Goldbarth: You were in your twenties at this time?

Kinnell: In my late teens. I had one teacher to whom I showed my poems, the poet Charles Bell. He helped and encouraged me a great deal. He remains my closest friend and the person to whom I send my poems when I first write them.

Goldbarth: Do you still feel any insecurity about showing your work?

Kinnell: Then, I didn't know if I *could* write poems. I knew that was the only thing I wanted to do, but I didn't have the slightest idea whether or not I could actually do it. . . . It was a question of life or death to me. If I couldn't do it, I felt there was nothing for me in life at all. That was the reason for the insecurity.

Goldbarth: Did you have any trouble getting published when you were first starting?

Kinnell: Yes, I had a lot of trouble. And I hated having my poems turned down. Gradually I learned not to pay attention to what editors and publishers thought. And yet sooner or later there has to be some indication from the outside, to prevent self-confidence from turning into the delusion of grandeur, which it must do to keep itself from crumbling altogether. You need to have someone read your poem and say, "It's good." When Charles Bell said this to me, when I was nineteen, I walked home in a kind of strange near-delirium. I hadn't been sure up until then whether I was able to write words that could actually touch another person.

Gilbert: Do you feel you've done that service yourself, for younger poets?

Kinnell: I'm not sure if the people I speak with feel that need quite so desperately. People who write poetry no longer work in such isolation. But the memory of how important that moment was stays with me and makes me know it's useful to teach.

Gilbert: Friends of mine complain that many student poets don't, as you did, want to reach out and touch somebody.

Kinnell: That might reflect a different conception of what poetry is; poetry as self-expression, or something. But if it's that others have seen and have liked their work all along and as a result they feel more assured and less worried about it, I would say they're lucky. To be free of that dread, you know, that fear of being deluded, is great good fortune.

Gilbert: Well, that loneliness you say you wrote out of—do you think that young poets today are less rich because they lack that?

Kinnell: I never thought of it as richness.

Gilbert: I meant richness for poetry.

Kinnell: I suppose everyone who writes is lonely. I doubt if it's useful to make them more so. But I see what your question implies. It *is* necessary to accept the loneliness, to lose one's dread of it. Without the loneliness there can be no poetry.

Goldbarth: Your "Correspondence School Instructor" poem—is that based on actual experience?

Kinnell: Yes. In the late fifties I taught a correspondence school course for the University of Chicago for a couple of years. There was loneliness! The people who took the course were in isolation wards, so to speak, little towns across the country, where they had nobody to whom they could show their poems. I felt very useful, teaching the course, but it was very painful as well to be the one listening.

Goldbarth: If I told you this was going to be the last statement you could make in this interview, what would you say?

Kinnell: Well, I would say, I'm—I'm glad.

III

An Interview with Mary Jane Fortunato

New York City, Spring 1971

Fortunato: In our *New York Quarterly* craft interviews we have tried to be as objective as possible and not to get too involved with feelings and emotions about things, but stay with craft and style.

Kinnell: Matters I don't know anything about.

Fortunato: Could you tell us something about your method of writing—revision and that sort of thing?

Kinnell: I often write a first draft of a poem rather quickly. Sometimes I revise quite a lot.

Fortunato: And what about beginning to write at a certain time of the day, music?

Kinnell: I don't really have habits, or habits of that kind.

Fortunato: What about revising something that has already been published?

Kinnell: Yes, sometimes after a poem has come out in a magazine I might change it a bit here and there before putting it in a book. And I'm not above changing it even after it's in a book. But once a certain time has elapsed, it becomes impossible to add anything. The poem rejects the transplant. The most I can do then is to cut out the dead matter—which sometimes turns out to be the whole poem.

Fortunato: And your translations—your translations of François Villon—what function do you feel that translation has for a poet?

Kinnell: For the reader, you want to make the poem accessible. For yourself it's a way of getting really close, under the skin of a poem you admire. When you translate a poet, you invite or dare that poet to influence you. In my case I think one can see Bonnefoy in *Flower Herding* and possibly shades of Villon in *Body Rags*.

Fortunato: What about your recommendations regarding translations?

Kinnell: I think there are a few principles. The first would be too obvious to state except that it's almost never honored. It is that a translation ought to be accurate. It should render the sense, at least. If a translation does that, it can't be a complete failure. I've always liked the Penguin anthologies, the ones that have a prose translation at the bottom of the page. They are extremely useful if you know the language somewhat, and they *feel* trustworthy when you don't know it at all. Anyway, the world is small. We really do want to know as much as we can of what a poet in some other time or place actually thought and felt. It's maddening to have to wonder at practically every image, "Is this Neruda, or is this Ben Belitt?"

Another principle would be that, at least with poems that are difficult or obscure, the translation should be a little clearer than the original. Because of its verbal authority a poem can hold in suspension a number of possible meanings. A translation that tries to express the same ambiguity often ends up merely fuzzy or confused. It looks as though the translator had translated word for word a passage he didn't understand. A translation is an interpretation. The translator must decide what is the primary sense and say it rather clearly.

By accuracy, you see, I don't mean turning phrases in one language directly into phrases in another. The translator should assimilate the poem. So that when he makes the translation it is as if he expresses his own experience. I think that's the only way a poem can come into another language with any intensity or presence. Robert Fitzgerald's Homer has this experienced, assimilated feeling; so do Alastair Reid's translations of Neruda.

Fortunato: How do you feel about teaching in terms of what it does for your own work?

Kinnell: Teaching is exciting and interesting, in itself, and it is an honorable profession. But if one does too much of it and it becomes a chore, it can be depressing and bad for a writer. The worst thing about teaching is that it puts you in contact mostly with people preoccupied by the things that preoccupy you. It would be better to find a work by which you could enter a world different from your own, in its people, materials, and terminology.

Fortunato: What about the relationship between poetry and education? Is there enough poetry in it?

Kinnell: I doubt if the way poetry is usually taught in colleges is the right way. Of course, I wouldn't like it *not* taught in colleges either. And yet if you're at all moved or affected when you read a poem, you might want to remain silent just then. In a class you've got to talk. And if you're not able to understand fully a poem that fascinates you, maybe it would be better simply to read it again and again, get it by heart, and slowly come around to an understanding that might for a long time remain inexpressible in words. In a class you must take the poem apart, paraphrase its meaning, identify its tone, structure, metaphors, poetic devices, and so on, and do all this, usually, in someone else's critical language.

Fortunato: Would there be another way to present poetry to a class?

Kinnell: Ideally, only ancient poetry should be studied in universities. The function of the study would be simply to compensate for the time that has gone by. Contemporary poetry, being part of one's own surroundings, wouldn't need any study. This isn't how it is, partly because poetry is *not* part of our surroundings, but also because some of the best known twentieth-century poetry is peculiarly difficult and probably does require some sort of exegesis. But perhaps we should try to discover another way of teaching modern poems. Perhaps we shouldn't teach them directly but should use them as texts in courses about other things—about ourselves, about those inner experiences most of us learn to discount and ignore until we no longer have them. This sounds like an encounter group, or a third-grade introduction-to-poetry class—and probably it would end up that way.

Fortunato: Do you think we have failed to create an audience for poetry in the basic education system—not just in the colleges? Do you think it should be a spontaneous thing—and if not created do you think it should just die?

Kinnell: I think the return of poetry to the schools is part of the widespread, "spontaneous" reaction against technological civilization and not something forcibly imposed by educators and committees. Probably those who do "create an audience" for poetry are themselves moved by the same need they look for in the students.

Fortunato: You say you have no habits, but how do you write?

Kinnell: Well, I never write on a typewriter. Sometimes I keep notebooks. Since I tend to lose them, I manage with scraps of paper.

Fortunato: Do you carry around a fragment or a line for ages until you see it in a poem?

Kinnell: Sometimes I do.

Fortunato: Is that your usual way of starting a poem?

Kinnell: You see, I don't really have a usual way. I've started some poems that way, and at times I've written the whole poem out from beginning to end.

Fortunato: About six years ago there was a photograph in *Life* magazine with regard to your involvement in civil rights. How do you feel about involvement in any political activity for a poet?

Kinnell: Poets may feel freer than most people to support unpopular causes. It isn't that there won't be consequences. Tom McGrath, for instance, was blacklisted by the colleges for years, and Robert Mezey lost several jobs for objecting, before the rest of academia, to our involvement in Vietnam. I doubt if poetry can come from a person who feels nothing for others, who can't imagine someone else's sufferings.

Fortunato: In terms of enriching your poetry, do you feel involvement has any bearing on that?

Kinnell: I think involvement in any life-giving effort, whether a cause or some private thing, like caring for a sick friend—any involvement that brings you to a sense of loving community purifies and is bound to be enriching—for a writer or for anyone.

Fortunato: What about your poems "The Bear" and "The Porcupine"? They have been interpreted as rather unique nature poems. Do you agree with this?

Kinnell: I don't think the distinction between "nature poem" and "urban poem" is useful any longer. The idea that we and our creations don't belong to "nature" comes from the notion that the human is a special being created in God's image to have dominion over all else. We are becoming aware again of our connection with other beings. That's hopeful, since for several centuries our civilization has done all it could to forget it.

Fortunato: So this isn't a totally new development?

Kinnell: There was Thoreau, for example. Though he loved building, improvising, fixing things, his aversion to the technological spirit was like an allergy. Most other nineteenth-century figures happily rode the wave of the future. It gave Thoreau hives of the soul. He was a kind of evolutionary mutation, a new man we have yet to catch up with, who sickens in the presence of the will to detach, objectify, and dominate.

Fortunato: He was the first?

Kinnell: I suppose that in human societies from the beginning, there was both a drive to control and dominate the rest of life, and also a desire to be one with the rest. These opposing urges must have been in reasonable balance, often both must have been present in the same act, of hunting, cultivation, propitiation, and so on. Since the Renaissance the drive to dominate has won out.

Fortunato: What do you do about dry periods? Do you have them?

Kinnell: Yes, of course, but I don't think of them that way—more as complications of life—usually practical but also emotional—which make me too busy to write or uninterested in writing.

Fortunato: So you wait as you simplify and it just levels off? Then you write again.

Kinnell: So it's been in the past. May it be so in the future.

Fortunato: Do you think it is necessary for a poet to go through a form and then break out of it?

Kinnell: That was what happened to my generation. Almost all of us began writing in strict forms. Almost all of us sooner or later turned to free verse. I doubt if this will happen in the future. I think those of my age who say you have to "learn the rules in order to break them" are wrong to generalize from their own experience. That experience was a historical quirk. I don't think it's useful for all who follow to repeat it. Young poets seem to do very well writing in free verse. I don't imagine there will be much of a return to form. But who knows? A number of fine poets—Richard Wilbur, Etheridge Knight, James Merrill, Donald Justice, to name four—never did completely give up form. And this very minute the great poets to come may be honing their villanelles.

Fortunato: Do you ever set up a form and try to write within it for a challenge?

Kinnell: There are too many challenges already that I can't avoid. I don't want to invent more.

Fortunato: Your long poem, "The Avenue Bearing the Initial of Christ into the New World"—was it your intention at that time to write a long poem?

Kinnell: Yes, I understood from the first that it would be a long poem. It rather wrote itself and it surprised me not so much by its length as by the sudden way it all seemed to come together and be finished.

IV

An Interview with
A. Poulin, Jr., and Stan Sanvel Rubin

Brockport, New York, November 1971

First Song

Then it was dusk in Illinois, the small boy
After an afternoon of carting dung
Hung on the rail fence, a sapped thing
Weary to crying. Dark was growing tall
And he began to hear the pond frogs all
Calling on his ear with what seemed their joy.

Soon their sound was pleasant for a boy
Listening in the smoky dusk and nightfall
Of Illinois, and from the fields two small
Boys came bearing cornstalk violins,
And they rubbed the cornstalk bows with rosins
And the three sat there scraping of their joy.

It was now fine music the frogs and the boys
Did in the towering Illinois twilight make,
And into dark in spite of a shoulder's ache
A boy's hunched body loved out of a stalk
The first song of his happiness, and the song woke
His heart to the darkness, and into the sadness of joy.

Poulin: Since "First Song" is the first poem in your first
book, *What a Kingdom It Was*, it elicits an obvious first
question. What kinds of impulses originally necessitated

your writing poetry and under what kinds of circumstances did you start writing?

Kinnell: I knew, from the age of twelve on, that writing poetry was what I wanted to do, but it wasn't until I was around eighteen that I began to write what you might call seriously. As for the impulses that set me writing, I remember I lived a kind of double life: my "public" life with everyone I knew—brother, sisters, parents, friends, and so on—and my secret life with the poems I would read late at night. I found my most intimate feelings were shared in those poems more fully than in the relationships I had in the world. I suppose I came to think that in poetry it might be possible to say the things I couldn't express in ordinary life.

Poulin: Do you recall what poems you were reading?

Kinnell: A lot of Poe. Also Dickinson, Shelley, Wordsworth, Kipling, Housman, even James Whitcomb Riley and Robert Service.

Rubin. Did you read Whitman early?

Kinnell: Yes, but I didn't understand him. It wasn't until I was in my mid-twenties that I really discovered him. Then I found him marvelous. It could be Whitman isn't a poet for young people. He's physical, but mystically physical. The young are both too down-to-earth, and too spiritual, to take to that. The teenager is almost gnostic in his dualism.

Poulin: Besides reading, what other kinds of events or experiences influenced your work? In his review of *What a Kingdom It Was*, James Dickey stated: "Perhaps to a degree more than is true of other poets, Kinnell's development will depend on the actual events of his life." How accurate was Dickey's prediction?

Kinnell: My poetry does stay fairly close to the experiences of my life. I don't usually write in others' voices. Probably this has come to be even more true in my last two books. My children, for example, appear often in *The Book of Nightmares.* I think in the book Dickey was reviewing a number of the poems were pure inventions—part of a series I wrote about how it might be to grow up on the Illinois prairie in the nineteenth century, of which "First Song" is one. So there was perhaps a certain prescience in his remark.

Poulin: But reading your poems one doesn't have the sense, as one does with more personal poets—Lowell, Plath, or Sexton—that this is an actual, real person speaking. There is always the sense of a kind of persona in the poem. I mean, one doesn't feel one's getting to know Galway Kinnell the private person.

Kinnell: That may be true, I don't know. But insofar as I use my own life in my poems I think of it as being much the same as others' lives. I change things, mostly to bring out something, but perhaps also to take away some detail that keeps it merely autobiographical.

Rubin: You've written that the poem comes in part out of the poet's desire to be changed, out of his struggle with his own nature. Is the death of the ego a recognizable point in a poem; is it a place you go through when you're writing a poem?

Kinnell: In some great poems, like "Song of Myself," a reader is taken through one person into some greater self;

there is a continual passing into the "death of the self," to use that phrase. It's one of the things that makes "Song of Myself" glorious. As we read this poem, we have to open ourselves if we are to get anything at all out of it. When we come to the lines "I was the man, I suffered, I was there," we already understand what it is to disappear into someone else. The final action of the poem, where Whitman dissolves into the air and into the ground, is for me one of the great moments of self-transcendence in poetry. In one way or another, consciously or not, all poems try to pass beyond the self. The best poems are those in which you are not this or that person, but anyone, just a person. If you could go farther, you would no longer be a person but an animal. If you went farther still you would be the grass, eventually a stone. If a stone could speak your poem would be its words.

Rubin: That makes me think of the topic of death which runs throughout your poetry.

Kinnell: Yes, as death has two aspects—the extinction, which we fear, and the flowing away into the universe, which we desire—there is a conflict within us that I want to deal with.

Rubin: It also seems to me that you almost feel at times that the moment of death is the moment of heightened clinging to life. I know you've written about Emily Dickinson's "I Heard a Fly Buzz When I Died."

Kinnell: Yes, I think that's what Emily Dickinson was doing when she wrote the poem—imagining the heightened feeling she would have for the world when she left it. The last section of *The Book of Nightmares* was written in something of that spirit.

Rubin: This is something then that we should be able to do continuously?

Kinnell: Many think we should forget about death. Much of contemporary culture is devoted to helping us do this. But I like what Hegel says: "The life of the spirit is not frightened at death and does not keep itself pure of it. It lives with death and maintains itself in it." Yves Bonnefoy uses this as the epigraph to his wonderful book, *On the Motion and Immobility of Douve*.

Poulin: I find myself disagreeing with both of you. My reading of *The Book of Nightmares* suggests an equal strain of transcendence of some kind. There's a profound traditional religious attitude toward death; if not life after death, then at least some form of transcendence both in the newer poems as well as in the earlier ones.

Kinnell: I think that about halfway through my first book I ceased to look for that traditional kind of transcendence. Certain poems in the last half of the book are explicit struggles to be rid of such a desire. But such desires run deep and perhaps the most we can do is disguise them.

Poulin: You said once that "the dream of every poem is to be a myth," and I wonder if any orthodox mythology is viable today, and if not, what then are the materials of a more contemporary myth.

Kinnell: I doubt if old myths, born at other times, in other cultures, can be very much alive for us. When I said that, I don't know if I meant myth in the usual sense. Perhaps I meant that the poem is a kind of paradigm of what the human being wants to say to the cosmos. The old myths were a bit like that. This is what John Logan has in mind when he speaks of poetry's "sacramental character."

Rubin: Your poem, "The Dead Shall Be Raised Incorruptible," has perhaps more of what might be termed political content, social content, than almost any of your other poems. What motivated that poem?

Kinnell: I wrote that poem out of the same obsessive concerns that have led almost every poet in this country to turn to political subjects. Many of the poems we wrote were terrible, but they had to be written. My own poem fails in some ways, but it did force me to try to understand certain things, such as what has become of us that we can kill on a vast scale and not even be able to say why.

Rubin: I asked you that because it is a kind of exception in *The Book of Nightmares*, and yet it clearly relates to the nightmare you're speaking of. It's not the way you normally write or the kind of theme you normally handle.

Kinnell: That's probably true, although in the previous book there is a poem called "The Last River" which is as political, and a good deal longer. You see, what I wanted to do in *The Book of Nightmares* in regard to politics, as well as in regard to other elements that come into the poem, was to bring from the central core of the poem a sort of light onto—well, I could say onto any subject whatever. I wanted it to be that any one of those ten sections could have been about anything at all.

This light would bind each unconnected thing into the wholeness of the poem.

Poulin: What, exactly, would you say, is that central core?

Kinnell: I was afraid you might ask me that!

Poulin: Why do you think so many poets have been working on long poems and sequences recently?

Kinnell: The desire for a poem in which you can say everything, in which there is nothing that has to be left out.

Poulin: That's very close to what Ginsberg is trying to do and, of course, it recalls Whitman, doesn't it—to include the entire universe?

Kinnell: I suppose that Ezra Pound has had the most influence on the way the long poem has developed. For myself, while I want a poem that can include everything, I don't yet want to abandon what I think of as organic form—where the poem isn't made by accretion, by adding lines and stanzas, sections and books, and so on, indefinitely, as *Paterson* and the *Cantos* were made. I still want a long poem to be an organism: to be born, to grow, to come to a certain fullness and climax, and to end. It may be in the future I will want to write a flat poem, without boundaries, a kind of medieval wandering—I don't rule that out.

Rubin: While reading *The Book of Nightmares*, which I did read as one poem—I couldn't put it down because the voice was continuous and gripping—I felt that something's happened to your relationship with time. I don't know how, perhaps your children may have something to do with that.

Kinnell: What do you feel has happened?

Rubin: A sense that a particular kind of affirmation of natural life that one gets reading your earlier poems is somewhat modulated here. Even in the opening poem, "Under the Maud Moon," there is a real consciousness of time-future I think, in a way that I don't precisely sense in your earlier work. For example, the last image in the book: "see if you can find the one flea which is laughing." Somehow that's a little more tentative than, say, the poem "The Fly."

Kinnell: Perhaps. For myself, *The Book of Nightmares*, for all that tentative and fearful quality you correctly see in it, is as affirmative as anything I've written. I'm the last person to be able to judge such things, of course. It's true that throughout the poem there is a harping on transience. In earlier poems it's not quite so constant, and there's usually an effort to make it seem all right. There is one early poem, "Spindrift," in which the final—and seventh—section reads,

> What does he really love,
> That old man,
> His wrinkled eyes
> Tortured by smoke,
> Walking in the ungodly
> Rasp and cackle of old flesh?
>
> The swan dips her head
> And peers at the mystic
> In-life of the sea,
> The gull drifts up
> And eddies toward heaven,
> The breeze in his arms . . .

27

Nobody likes to die
But an old man
Can know
A kind of gratefulness
Towards time that kills him,
Everything he loved was made of it.

I like this passage; I don't disavow it in any way. But I have grown older—the poem was written about 1960—and, more crucially, there have come into my life two children, as you say. It would be nice if in a single poem one could resolve a given problem forever—come to terms with it once and for all. But each poem comes out of its own moment. In *The Book of Nightmares* I seem to face time's passing as if for the first time. It is bound up now with the twin fears that parents of small children feel, the fear of losing the children and the fear of leaving them. I hoped the flea of the last line wouldn't sound *quite* so tentative. I had been thinking, you see, that fleas on the body of a happy person would be a bit happier than other fleas.

Poulin: In your essay, "The Poetics of the Physical World," you spoke of the dichotomy between the "poetics of heaven" and the "poetics of the physical world." But in *The Book of Nightmares* you seem to have managed a reconciliation between them.

Kinnell: I came to feel very free in writing that poem. I felt I could set down the very worst, anything, no matter what. I could evoke in the poem the most revolting presences. I could do this in total faith that something was sustaining the whole poem that would not allow it to be a record of self-disgust, or hatred of nature, or fear of death, or loneliness, or defeat, but rather ultimately a restorative and healing and, if I can use the word, a happy poem.

Poulin: There's been a great change in the structure of your poems from *What a Kingdom It Was* to *The Book of Nightmares* and I'm rather fascinated by some of them. In "The Poetics of the Physical World," you say that for the modern poet rhyme and meter, having lost their sacred meaning and natural basis, amount to little more than mechanical aids for writing. First of all I'm intrigued by why they've lost their sacred and natural basis for the modern poet or for you.

Kinnell: Oh, I'm just guessing. I guess that the Elizabethans, for instance, sensed some lovely repetitiveness about existence. The rhymes in their poems are a way of acknowledging the everlasting return of things. A harmony sounded through time. The formal aspects of their poems were ways of sharing in it, perhaps of propitiating it. Most of us moderns hear nothing like that. When we listen we hear outer space telling us we're a race living for a while on a little planet that will die. As for what lies beyond, we know nothing—our brains are the wrong kind, or are too small, or something. When the astronauts looked back at the earth, what they felt most keenly was its fragility. The seasons do return, but now with poignancy, because almost nothing else does.

Rubin: You quote from C. M. Bowra's *Primitive Songs* in several places. What do those kinds of poems mean to you?

Kinnell: I quoted a few of those poems hoping they would serve as contrasts to nineteenth-century English poetry, the conventions of which dominate our conception of poetry and even define the "poetic" way to feel about things. The poems from *Primitive Songs*, partly, perhaps, because they're in plain translations, seem psychologically more true.

Rubin: Is this a good place for poets generally to go then?

Kinnell: I think so. We need other sources besides conventional English poetry. There are absolutely glorious poems in this tradition, of course, and anyone who wants to write will know them. But to steep oneself exclusively in this tradition, as many do, isn't a good idea. Precisely because the tradition is so attractive, all those "poetic," distorting qualities take a fierce hold on you and suddenly you discover it is hard to get rid of them. It's a good idea to read poets who are a little out of main tradition—like Smart, Blake, Dickinson, Tuckerman, Clare, Melville. And poetry in another language is also good, in the original, and in translations that don't try to be conventional English poems themselves.

Rubin: Perhaps a poem like "In Memoriam"—one of those big sloppy poems which I don't think you or very many readers have much affection for—is in a sense a kind of parallel to *The Book of Nightmares* in terms of Tennyson's attempt to work out his unanswerable questions.

Kinnell: It's not a poem that moves me very much, but it's one that I respect. It's rare to find a poet who at least tries to confront, in all its moral and intellectual complexity, some very personal and painful event. I don't think the poem succeeds—in part perhaps because of its decorative form, which I think discourages Tennyson from expressing his ragged, unpoetic, "rhymeless" perceptions.

Poulin: Would you care to discuss what you're currently working on beyond *The Book of Nightmares*?

Kinnell: I thought of that poem as one in which I could say everything that I knew or felt. Now that it's finished, now that some time has passed since it's been finished, I see that it wasn't everything. But still I don't quite know what I shall write. Just now I'm writing some prose criticism. I do feel tired. I have to wait until I feel an energy that wants to come out in words.

Rubin: Might you be relieved in some way if you didn't feel the same sort of need that motivated *The Book of Nightmares*?

Kinnell: I don't think so. I didn't want to let that poem go. I felt I could spend the rest of my life writing it— revising and perfecting it. So I held on to it. Eventually I had to force myself to get rid of it, though I knew I would feel an unsettling emptiness for a long time afterward. I hope I feel as totally consumed again.

Rubin: Does that mean you don't feel that the writing of prose makes the same sort of demands on you?

Kinnell: No, I don't. Prose criticism is mostly the working out and setting down of opinions.

Poulin: In the course of our conversation you've agreed that traditional mythology and symbology are no longer viable; you suggested that the formal and inner conventions of poetry must be discarded; and in "The Poetics of the Physical World" you state that formal beauty is an impediment to the discovery of glory. I wonder, what is there left?

Kinnell: Besides all those things I foolishly threw out? I don't know. But maybe it's as well to leave all that. Maybe the fewer conventions or guides we have, the more chance there is to come to some new place. Rather than writing merely competent, conventional poems, I imagine it's better to do something more bold, even though it may turn out to be awful, if it seems that in that way lies a possibility of finding that great thing you may be after.

Poulin: While thanking you, may I also ask you to read "Last Songs" which seems to complement the start as well as much of the substance of this conversation?

Last Songs

1

What do they sing, the last birds
coasting down the twilight,
banking
across woods filled with darkness, their
frayed wings
curved on the world like a lover's arms
which form, night after night, in sleep,
an irremediable absence?

2

Silence. Ashes
in the grate, Whatever it is
that keeps us from heaven,
sloth, wrath, greed, fear, could we only
reinvent it on earth
as song.

Edited from a prose transcription of a videotape interview with Galway Kinnell in November, 1971, sponsored by the Brockport Writers Forum, Department of English, State University College, Brockport, N.Y. 14420. All rights reserved, State University of New York.

V

An Interview with James J. McKenzie

Grand Forks, North Dakota, 1972

McKenzie: This is your sixth poetry reading in as many days, and you have three more to go. In spite of the obvious rigors of such an experience, do you enjoy reading on a poetry circuit?

Kinnell: I've learned to be careful on trips—I go to bed early, don't eat much, don't drink, and play tennis when I can. Every day I try to put in an hour or so of work. And, then, somehow, it seems OK. Anyway poetry readings aren't especially hard work. It's nice to be paid just to read one's poems aloud.

McKenzie: Do you feel that reading poetry in public places helps you with your poetry in any way?

Kinnell: I'm not sure. Sometimes I notice there are certain lines I don't feel like reading—something's wrong with them that I don't notice until I have to say them to an audience—though that happens so seldom it doesn't justify wandering around the country. Perhaps giving readings also affects the music of the poems—it may lengthen the lines, give them more flowing cadences. I suspect I'm just making up this idea! Probably the main thing it does that's useful is make one want to write more, so as to have something new to read. I remember when I was writing *The Book of Nightmares*, I'd work in hotel rooms, and read at night the lines I had written that day.

McKenzie: Do you often send poems off to friends around the country for criticism and suggestions before you reach the final version of the poem?

Kinnell: Yes, there are three or four people I send my poems to. Of course one never finds the person one can absolutely rely on. For me Charles Bell comes pretty close.

McKenzie: Could you talk a little about how a poem typically begins with you—or isn't there any typical beginning?

Kinnell: There isn't any typical way. Sometimes an experience produces a poem. Sometimes words appear before I know what they mean or where they might lead. Sometimes I conceive of the whole poem without knowing any of its words.

McKenzie: Could you talk about the genesis of a specific poem, perhaps—how, say, "Another Night in the Ruins" began?

Kinnell: Well, I had bought an old ruined house in Vermont. It didn't have windows or doors and the roof was falling in. I went up there in winter once—I went in on skis, put plastic sheeting on some windows, lit the stove I'd put in that fall, and stayed awhile. One night I stayed up all night mainly because I was too cold to sleep, and wrote a number of disconnected fragments, some descriptive of the place, some imagined, some memories. I threw away most of them and kept seven, which I then strung together to make the poem.

McKenzie: But did it begin with a notion of the whole poem?

Kinnell: No, it didn't. It began as pieces.

McKenzie: Did that poem reach its final stages in that one night?

Kinnell: No, I worked a great deal on the last section. It was about a year before I finished it.

McKenzie: I wonder if maybe you could talk a little about the genesis of *The Book of Nightmares*. At what point in your working with that sequence did you know you were going to do a whole book-length poem? Did you begin with a few poems or did you have a conception of the whole thing from the beginning?

Kinnell: I began it as a single ten-part sequence. I had been rather immersed in the *Duino Elegies*. In the Ninth Elegy, Rilke says, in effect, "Don't try to tell the angels about the glory of your feelings, or how splendid your soul is; they know all about that. Tell them something they'd be more interested in, something that you know better than they, tell them about the things of the world." So it came to me to write a poem called "The Things." Like the *Elegies* it would be a poem without plot, yet with a close relationship among the parts, and a development from beginning to end. I did write a draft of that entire poem one spring, while I was living in Seattle. I didn't like it and I threw it away, almost all of it. One of the surviving passages became "The Hen Flower." Then I started again. The poem has moved far from its original intention to be about things and now probably does try to tell the angels about the glory of my feelings!

McKenzie: Did you have to labor to finish it or did it come pretty easily?

Kinnell: Not easily. It took four years. A lot of that time I worked on it day after day. While I was in Spain I worked on it almost every day for six hours or so, not writing, of course, all that time, but working on it.

McKenzie: Do you feel that *The Book of Nightmares* represents some kind of breakthrough for you, some discovery of a new method or form in which you will write now? Do you think you may, for example, write mostly in long sequences now?

Kinnell: The long poem has always been interesting to me. Even in college, I was writing longish poems. While this is certainly longer than anything else I've written, it's not formally very different from other poems—from the "Avenue C" poem, for example, or "The Last River." And yet it was an adventure of another kind— I felt in this poem free to speak of everything, to relate all areas of my life. As for what kind of poem I'll write in the future, I haven't any idea.

McKenzie: Whitman is someone that sooner or later almost every American poet feels that he has to come to terms with.

Kinnell: Yes, though of course few have done so.

McKenzie: Do you accept the notion that there are two main strands of American poetry: the academic and the nonacademic; or as some people call them, "pale face and red skin"? Whitman being among the latter?

Kinnell: Well, it's not very useful to talk about American poetry in terms of two kinds. Most of those who use those terms, academic and nonacademic, think of the Black Mountain Poets, for example, as being "nonacademic," yet most of these poets have no connection at all with Whitman, even less connection than someone like Robert Lowell who, I guess, would be an "academic." Our poetry is so eclectic, so crossbred, so subject to stray influence, that it's pointless to classify it. Whitman does belong to a specific tradition, though—he had a few ancestors—whom he never read—and until very recently, only a few descendents.

McKenzie: Another American poet who comes to my mind when you talk about the way one uses the surface of things is William Carlos Williams. Do you think that he's in the Whitman tradition as you have been describing it?

Kinnell: You'd think he would be. But for most of his life he tended to be what I would call "photographic." Whitman's adjective enters the thing and feels out some inner quality, while Williams tends to use the straight descriptive word. For example, in his little poem, "So much depends/upon/a red wheelbarrow . . ." we see the scene but we don't experience it. Without its first line—which is to say without its idea—the poem might not be interesting. Perhaps the Williams dictum, "No ideas but in things," in practice actually means, "No things but in ideas," as it seems to in the red wheelbarrow poem. Later in his life, when he could write in long, comfortable, cadenced lines, often much like quite loose blank verse, as in the "Asphodel" poem, he comes closer to Whitman.

McKenzie: Denise Levertov in talking about her writing methods cited you as someone whose methods were quite different from hers.

Kinnell: Yes.

McKenzie: She said that you seem to labor over poems and throw out a great deal, whereas she thought that she herself didn't revise as much as you do and didn't tend to cut out as much. Do you care to talk about this?

Kinnell: I don't know that I can say very much. She's told me that when she's going to write a poem she waits until it's fully formed, then writes it down and changes no more than a few words afterward. This sometimes happens to me, but more often I struggle. Perhaps it's because her feelings, her understandings, are extremely clear—or so they've always struck me. By contrast, I always seem to be floundering. My poems are more like the acts of one who is lost.

McKenzie: The other day partly as a result of reading your book, we were wondering about a curious phenomenon. Although many poets are connected with universities, it seems almost impossible to write a poem about university life in our age. It seemed to us that the university drives poets into deliberately seeking out other kinds of experiences, such as direct contact with nature, for their poems. Do you feel those pressures as a teacher and a poet?

Kinnell: In the university, it's a particularly modern kind of life, because you don't really know what makes it go. It's like riding an elevator. It's the wrong place for a poet to live. You should live more naturally, which is to say both more in harmony and more at odds with what's around you.

McKenzie: Was there a time in your life when you lived away from the university and do you feel that these experiences were important to you as a young poet? I know a lot of your early poems deal with hunting and rural life.

Kinnell: I started out teaching for a few years, and here I am teaching again. In between I spent probably twelve years picking up my living as I could. I took odd jobs here and there, and I was also thrifty enough to be able to spend years without a job. I'm thankful I didn't spend all that time on a campus. In the last five years I've taught a semester here, a semester there, sporadically. At least half of the time in the last five years I haven't been teaching. I guess what I would *not* like to do is teach in a small college, live near the campus, have all my friends be professors, and so on. I love teaching, but I prefer to do it without being totally absorbed into campus life.

McKenzie: Do you ever teach any literature courses or do you mostly do creative writing courses?

Kinnell: No, they don't seem to trust me to teach anything but a poetry workshop.

McKenzie: Are you ever drawn to work in some other *genre*, or another medium? You have one novel, for example; do you plan more?

Kinnell: I don't know. I hadn't really planned to write that novel. It came about through particular circumstances. It could happen again. Life is short, however, and novels are long.

McKenzie: How about theater? Has it ever occurred to you to attempt a play?

Kinnell: I used to feel I couldn't write for the theater. It had something to do with my sense of time. I felt I didn't understand time in the way needed for the theater. I don't know if that's true. I think I might like to write a film script, where the images take care of time.

McKenzie: But you haven't really pursued that notion any further?

Kinnell: No.

VI

An Interview with
Wayne Dodd and Stanley Plumly

Athens, Ohio, May 15, 1972

Interviewer: We were speaking of poetry readings. I wonder, do you think that for your poetry, as you conceive it, the printed page is essential?

Kinnell: Yes, it is. We forget. The printed page is our memory. And how magical that from those squiggles can arise an actual physical cadence and music.

Interviewer: Why is *The Book of Nightmares* so symmetrical—ten poems, seven parts each?

Kinnell: That there are ten sections is in tribute to the *Duino Elegies*, and I had already been writing poems in seven parts. . . .

Interviewer: Yes, "The Porcupine," for example.

Kinnell: And these too started coming out in seven parts. Some, of course, could as easily have been in eight or six parts. I just brought them all into seven parts.

Interviewer: How important is narrative for your work, your poetry?

Kinnell: Certain of my poems, like "The Avenue Bearing the Initial of Christ into the New World" don't use narrative. Others do, like "The Bear." I've felt recently that I'd like to write poems that teach, not by story or example, but by direct expression of ideas.

Interviewer: Do you think there would be any consequent loss of that sense of personal emotional involvement that inheres in the kind of narrative you do?

Kinnell: I think the danger would be that the poem might get a bit preachy.

Interviewer: When I asked the question about narrative I was thinking of a poem like "Freedom, New Hampshire," in which there are these narrative segments. Maybe the progression is another kind of progression, not a narrative progression, but narrative is the fundamental element out of which the units are constructed: each little narrative is itself the metaphor.

Kinnell: The little stories are, of course, the very material of that poem. It's only at the very end that the poem "teaches" in the sense I mean. It stops telling what once happened to this or that person, and turns to the reader and tries to generalize about what happens to us all.

Interviewer: You mentioned briefly Rilke's influence. How about Yeats? Your two children are named after Yeats, in effect, after the life surrounding Yeats. How does he come into your poetry?

Kinnell: In my early twenties I thought Yeats was not only the greatest of all poets, but also in a manner of speaking, poetry itself. In everything I wrote I tried to reproduce his voice. If my poems didn't sound like Yeats, I thought they weren't poetry. Of course I was the only one to hear the resemblance. Yeats became a more useful mentor when I began to see his limitations. I think my interest in the poem made of sections, of elements that don't come together until the end, probably derives from Yeats, from poems like "Among Schoolchildren." I've always loved how all the materials of that poem come back woven together and transformed. In this way Yeats's more complicated poems resemble the Platonic dialogue.

Interviewer: What is it that you find in Rilke, besides his ability to structure the long poem as he does it, that's so apparently influential and dynamic in your own life and work?

Kinnell: Rilke writes only what is for him a matter of life and death. There's nothing trivial, no bright chatter, no clever commentary. He writes at the limit of his powers. There are moments when he seems to write beyond the limit. His poetry gropes out into the inexpressible, like the late music of Beethoven.

Interviewer: Can we return to the past, and get very personal? I have a sense when I read *The Book of Nightmares* that somehow or other that poem shares its genesis with that of your children: the fact of their birth and developing life is a very crucial, essential part of it. Is that right?

Kinnell: Yes.

Interviewer: Was that a part, really of your conceiving

of the thing—when you first began to think of the poem—as something that you were conscious of their life having brought you to?

Kinnell: When the poem began I knew the first section would be about birth, in particular the birth of my daughter, Maud. I didn't know until later, when Fergus was born, and the form of the whole began to come clear, that the last section would include a description of his birth too. The two births are the framework of the poem.

Interviewer: Hasn't your sense of the transience of human life—always so strong in your poetry—become more intense?

Kinnell: That's true. . . . Those little lumps of clinging flesh, and one's terrible, inexplicable closeness to them, make one feel very strongly the fragility of a person. In the company of babies, one is very close to the kingdom of death. And as children grow so quickly, as they change almost from day to day, it's hardly possible to put mortality out of mind for long.

Interviewer: *The Book of Nightmares* is dedicated to your children, and it seems to me a book for children. You just spoke of Rilke's *Duino Elegies* as teaching poems—I see that intention also in *The Book of Nightmares*. There's that instructional quality: "I'm going to introduce you to this tragic sense, this understanding of *duende*, that your life is going to become."

Kinnell: I wanted that book, while it introduces these things, to suggest a way of dealing with them.

Interviewer: Absolutely. That's what I meant by instruction: "If you know this, if you learn this. . . ." The Maud poem, the first poem, ends with, "And then/you shall open/this book, even if it is the book of nightmares." Still you leave it as an affirmative poem.

Kinnell: *I* think so. Though I know many feel the strong negative force in the poem. There's really nothing I can point to, to argue the matter—it's so much a matter of feeling. I could mention Greek or Shakespearean tragedy: much of what is actually said is destructive, yet the total effect is the contrary. What it is that brings happiness is not ever entirely expressed in the words.

Interviewer: You have as an epigraph to *The Book of Nightmares* a quotation from Rilke:

> But, this though: death,
> the whole of death—even before life's begun,
> to hold it all so gently, and be good:
> this is beyond description!

How do you see the relationship of this epigraph to your book?

Kinnell: This passage appears after the dedication to Maud and Fergus. From one point of view, the book is nothing but an effort to face death and live with death. Children have all that effort in their future. They have glimpses of death through fatigue, sleep, cuts and bruises, warnings, etc., and also through their memory of the nonexistence they so recently came from. They seem to understand death surprisingly clearly. But now time passes slowly for them. It hardly exists. They live with death almost as animals do. This natural trust in life's rhythms, infantile as it is, provides the model for the trust they may struggle to learn later on. *The Book of Nightmares* is my own effort to find the trust again. I invoke Maud and Fergus not merely to instruct them, but also to get help from them.

Interviewer: When I read your poems—the ones I like best—I sense that you manage to charge them with a total emotional intensity, and that then that emotional tension is discharged in an emotional, not intellectual resolution. It has something to do with their being dramatic, with their dramatizing of some narrative event. And also with the size of the poem. It has to be a longish poem to do that, perhaps. Do you have any theory about that, or any perspective on it in retrospect?

Kinnell: Well, not really. I suppose the emotional intensity is related to the time spent wandering or struggling—before the poem comes to a resolution. Short poems are more difficult for me than longer ones, and a bit frustrating, since I want the poem to have an inner drama. I want a poem to include time.

Interviewer: I find "The Hen Flower" to be the most individual poem in *The Book of Nightmares*—I'm not sure why. One reason, perhaps, is that it's self-addressed: you're the only character in it except for the hen, and yet, it seems to hold the resolution of all concerns of *The Book of Nightmares*. I guess my question is why is it in the second position?

Kinnell: The arrangement of *The Book of Nightmares* isn't entirely rational and it isn't entirely explicable. "The Hen Flower" was the first poem I finished of the sequence. It expresses the dread that is the poem's starting point. It addresses the protagonist before he begins the journey of the poem, instructing him to let go, to surrender to existence.

Interviewer: Who do you think you are most like in your handling of free verse, if anyone? You are without question a person very much in the old free verse tradition.

Kinnell: Well, as for influences, I don't know of any poetry whose music has moved me as much as that of Whitman; also the King James Bible.

Interviewer: In a recent essay you talk about how we need the mimetic quality of the human voice in a relationship with the raggedness of experience. Is that what you get from Whitman? That sense that this is a very human voice and has the openness of line and that all things are possible in this poem?

Kinnell: Yes. Whitman seeks in the music of his verse what he calls the "perfect rectitude and insouciance of the movements of animals" and his lines have that—they are exactly right yet there's no way to systemize them. Some of his most wonderful lines are rhythmically his oddest, the least systematic—"Let the cow, the horse, the camel, the garden-bee—let the mud-fish, the lobster, the mussel, eel, the sting-ray, and the grunting pig-fish— let these, and the like of these, be put on a perfect equality with man and woman!" All that is a single line. It's written in what could only be called the rhythm of what's being said.

Interviewer: The rhythm of what's being said?

Kinnell: A rhythm that's so expressive that one could take away the words and still almost convey the whole meaning. Infants and mothers do something like this when they croon to each other. They use rhythms alone and yet understand each other perfectly.

Interviewer: You once spoke of Ginsberg's "Howl" as being important to you.

Kinnell: Yes. I feel Ginsberg is the only one to understand Whitman and to bring into the poetry of our time a comparable music.

Interviewer: Yet, although you sweep the page, it's not an onslaught like Whitman or "Howl." Your line is kinetic, has much more a sense of break—angular or bony, or something. But it moves to extremes rapidly—the long line and suddenly you break to one word.

Kinnell: There are great differences in what Ginsberg and I each took from Whitman.

Interviewer: At the end of *Nightmares* you say something in the Fergus poem, "if this is a poem . . . "

Kinnell: "This poem, if we shall call it that."

Interviewer: That seems to be calling into question what the poem is. Is that true? Are you doubting the whole sense of what a poem can do?

Kinnell: I suppose I meant something like what Whitman meant when he said, "who touches this touches a man."

Interviewer: It's not self-deprecating or anything?

Kinnell: No.

Interviewer: In this essay on you in *Alone with America*, Richard Howard says something about how your poetry resists these facile reductions to the organic metaphors of growth. And he says that you always, right in the early moments, articulated your concerns and your themes—all of which seems to me a very sensitive and sound observation. But even if that is true, I still wonder what you think about your growth toward this: some poetic idea or ideal you have for your poetry? For example, you spoke earlier about this pure poem: do you think you have matured or grown or changed radically as a poet or anything of that sort?

Kinnell: Whatever I do will be different from *The Book of Nightmares*. A door has been closed on something. It would be foolish to go on in the same way. I've never had that feeling quite so strongly as I have with this book. As for growth, or change, from the beginning there have been no abrupt departures in my poetry. It has changed, changed totally I sometimes think, but there aren't many visible seams. In all the changes, however, I've never had a clearly articulated ideal.

Interviewer: Did you and Merwin write poems when you were at Princeton and show them to each other?

Kinnell: Yes, we showed each other poems—though mine, by comparison, were crude. Even at nineteen Merwin was writing poems of extraordinary skill and grace. His sense of the richness of English, his ear for its music, were then, and remain now even in his leaner poems, superior to anyone's. He was the one who introduced me to Yeats's poetry—he arrived late one night, book in hand, and read Yeats to me until dawn.

Interviewer: Have you turned your hand seriously to fiction since *Black Light*?

Kinnell: No, I haven't, and I doubt if I will.

Interviewer: I suppose one could ask, had you turned seriously to fiction before *Black Light*?

Kinnell: Yes, I'd started several novels and finished one. The novel form had always interested me. But I gradually came to understand that poetry could say almost everything I wanted to say. I think of *Black Light* as more of a fable than a novel. I would rather write a poem than a novel—and try to increase the weight that a poem can carry.

Interviewer: I want to ask a question about the speaking voice in your poems, especially in *The Book of Nightmares*. Any time I read a James Wright poem I have a sense that there's no persona there at all, but Wright speaking directly—and I think this is true of a poet like Bly as well. But I still have the sense, even in *The Book of Nightmares*, that there is a hero in those poems, a character being created, as in a long story, and that he's going through certain experiences, and being confronted by certain tests, and that he will win or lose by the end of the story. Assuming he does lose, which he will in your poems, his life is being celebrated nevertheless.

Kinnell: It's hard for me to judge. I haven't consciously invented a protagonist or mask. Yet the act of writing a poem that one hopes will speak for others as well as oneself tends to create something like a persona. So Whitman becomes "a kosmos, one of the roughs." And even Wordsworth, in *The Prelude*, who tries to write accurate autobiography, becomes a kind of exemplary case. I wouldn't find it surprising if the same thing happened in *The Book of Nightmares*. But I don't think I'm any different in this regard from Wright and Bly.

Interviewer: Well, I know you've been asked often about your use at times of the odd word, the out-of-the-way-word. In one section of *The Book of Nightmares*, "The Dead Shall Be Raised Incorruptible," is the most striking instance of that in all your poetry. Very near the beginning of that poem there is just a succession of, to the rest of us, essentially unknown words.

Kinnell: Well, English is a rich language—we don't know half of its words and we use even fewer. Even our poets sometimes write in something close to Basic English. When I encounter an old word on the verge of extinction, which seems expressive, I feel excited. I can't help entertaining the possibility of rescuing it, of putting it to use again. That list is of words signifying waste of one kind or another.

Interviewer: Who is your favorite non-English poet? Or is there one?

Kinnell: Well, I think Neruda.

Interviewer: Did you come to Neruda fairly early?

Kinnell: No, I didn't. I guess it was when I first met my wife—about fifteen years ago. She's Spanish. She used to read and translate Spanish poetry for me. We went through a number of poems of Neruda and Miguel Hernandez.

Interviewer: I don't see any surrealism, fantasia, going on in any of the things you have done so far.

Kinnell: You're right. But the mystery of the world isn't apprehended only by surrealist poems. In this country, we have a rich tradition of evoking physical things, of giving the physical world actual presence. Our language has more physical verbs and more physical adjectives in it than most others, and so has a peculiar capacity to bring into presence the creatures and things that the world is made up of. If the things and creatures that live on earth don't possess mystery, then there isn't any. To touch this mystery requires, I think, love of the things and creatures that surround us: the capacity to go out to them so that they enter us, so that they are transformed within us, and so that our own inner life finds expression through them. The use of the term "inner life" means that one is not quite whole, that one has an inner life and an outer life, and they don't quite come together. In the purest poem the inner and outer meet. If a poem remains at a surrealistic level, possibly it means that no integration takes place, that the inner world and the outer world do not come together.

Interviewer: You don't use the simile, for example, much at all. What is it about it that you mistrust or distrust, that makes you eschew it?

Kinnell: I don't think things are often really like other things. At some level all things *are* each other, but before that point they are separate entities. Also, although they are common, as you say, in surrealist poetry, similes perhaps have the effect of keeping the irrational world under rational supervision. Perhaps the words "like" and "as if" draw a line through reality and say in effect, "Here we are no longer speaking of the real world—here we indulge our imaginations." As for naturalistic similes, I used to use them much more than

I do. Now I tend to imply the simile in the verb—i.e., "Swift has sailed into his rest," instead of "Swift like a ship has gone into the harbor of death" or whatever.

Interviewer: What is the "advantage," aesthetic or otherwise, of the long poem over the short lyric?

Kinnell: A short poem can come to rest on the last note of the music box, so to speak, and exist timelessly there. It's like floating, as opposed to swimming. Blake expressed the principle:

> To see a World in a Grain of Sand
> And a Heaven in a Wild Flower,
> Hold Infinity in the palm of your hand
> And Eternity in an hour.

The long poem has the lesser ambition of wanting to hold only time in the palm of the hand and only an hour in an hour. The strength of the long poem is its capacity to show a development, to show an experience in its stages. Therefore time is an essential part of it. And yet because a long poem can bring a series of experiences to a climax, and transfigure them, it also, in its own way, can transcend time. There is no doubt that a long poem can do many things that are difficult to do in short poems. The catalogues in Homer or in Smart or in Whitman stand in the long poem without any specific justification; by themselves they would be fragments. And perhaps long poems can more easily deal with complicated ideas. Probably poets often turn to the long poem for the wrong reasons. It's assumed—falsely—that there's a connection between length and magnitude; that there's something inherently "major" about the long poem as opposed to the short.

Interviewer: Don't you think that it comes in part from the sense that to keep doing that thing he has done so many times will not hold enough challenges, or surprises, for the poet?

Kinnell: Yes. I do think a person has to go through a lot of changes, as Yeats did, or as W. S. Merwin has— Merwin, who so far, incidentally, hasn't shown much interest in the long poem.

Interviewer: There's a contemporary of Yeats who also went through those kinds of changes, perhaps not as famously as Yeats—D. H. Lawrence. He's a poet much influenced by Rilke. With the animals of *Body Rags*, I wondered how familiar you are with Lawrence's *Birds, Beasts, and Flowers*?

Kinnell: Yes, Lawrence is among the great germinal poets of modern times. I love his love poems and animal poems; I like less the didactic and social ones.

Interviewer: What sort of thing in Lawrence is it that you find most attractive?

Kinnell: His best love poems move us so far into mystery. They turn into acts of cosmic adoration. In some of them love of one person passes into worship of sexuality itself, as in the great poem, "River Roses":

> By the Isar, in the twilight
> We were wandering and singing,
> By the Isar, in the evening
> We climbed the huntsman's ladder and sat swinging
> In the fir-tree overlooking the marshes,
> While river met with river, and the ringing
> Of their pale-green glacier water filled the evening.

By the Isar, in the twilight
We found the dark wild roses
Hanging red at the river; and simmering
Frogs were singing, and over the river closes
Was savour of ice and of roses; and glimmering
Fear was abroad. We whispered: "No one knows us.
Let it be as the snake disposes
Here in this simmering marsh."

In Rilke's poetry he *tells* us that it is good to go beyond the contentment of love. In Lawrence's poems—just as in the fifth section of "Song of Myself"—this going-beyond actually takes place as an experience. In Lawrence's animal poems, I like it that the animals remain animals yet take on a symbolic character too.

Interviewer: I can't think of a poet before Lawrence who was able to do that.

Kinnell: Maybe John Clare did with his ladybug. Or Christopher Smart with his cat.

Interviewer: It's funny what a new life Christopher Smart has had in the last ten or fifteen years. All sorts of people have rediscovered and reread him after his long obscurity.

Kinnell: Richard Howard is making an anthology of modern poetry which will include an older poem that each poet chooses as especially important to him. He says four or five people wanted to use the Cat Geoffrey section of "Jubilate Agno."

Interviewer: What would be your poem?

Kinnell: Well, I wanted to use Rilke's Ninth Elegy but

the translations are too unsatisfactory. I used a bit of "Song of Myself."

Interviewer: Do you see your bear or porcupine functioning as symbols—or are they simply part of a larger symbolic structure or "journey"?

Kinnell: For me those animals had no specific symbolic correspondence. I thought of them as animals. Of course I wasn't making zoological portraits. "The Porcupine" tries to establish explicit connections between us and porcupines. In both "The Porcupine" and "The Bear" the one speaking actually becomes the animal. Whenever we identify with some thing or some animal, it at once begins to represent us or some aspect of us, and so is on its way to becoming a symbol, even if exactly what it represents can't be specified.

Interviewer: I keep circling back to things—what is that talismanic sort of thing on the cover of *The Book of Nightmares*? Who did the drawings?

Kinnell: They're all from old books.

Interviewer: Woodcuts?

Kinnell: Yes.

Interviewer: I assume they're your idea?

Kinnell: Yes. Some of them are from alchemical texts, some from books on practical matters, like how to find water . . . .

Interviewer: Yes, the dowsing rod.

Kinnell: When I saw a reproduction of the woodcut that's used on the cover I knew I wanted it, though I hadn't yet figured out who those two little angels were who were drawing the words from the mouth of the man about to be devoured. I wrote the Library of Congress and asked if there was a copy in the United States of the original book in which the woodcut appeared. I was living in Iowa City at the time. They wrote back and said there was only one copy in this country, at the Medical Library in Iowa City. So I walked down the street and had it photographed.

VII

An Interview with
Students in a Writing Class
at the University of Vermont

Burlington, Vermont, January 22, 1974

Student: What about political poems—do they have any effect? Was Auden right, that poetry "makes nothing happen"?

Kinnell: Obviously, poetry makes something happen in an inner sense. Shakespeare, Blake, Keats, affect us forever. On occasion, in an outer sense too. A poem can focus on some social or political reality with great freedom and great precision. For example, Robert Bly's poem, "Counting Small-Boned Bodies," written at the time when the daily "body count" of the Viet Cong was being reported in the newspapers, has illuminated reality for what probably adds up to tens of thousands of people. The poem goes like this:

Let's count the bodies over again.

If we could only make the bodies smaller,
The size of skulls,
We could make a whole plain white with skulls in the moonlight!

If we could only make the bodies smaller,
Maybe we could get
A whole year's kill in front of us on a desk!

If we could only make the bodies smaller,
We could fit
A body into a finger-ring, for a keepsake forever.

This poem helps those who were baffled by their revulsion at the body count by extracting something of its chilling essence. That's the thing about a political poem—one must learn something from it, learn something about the political event, and if possible in the best poems, about oneself as well. Robert Duncan does this in his marvelous poem "Uprising," one of the earliest poems written against the Vietnam war. Here's a section of it:

... And men wake to see that they are used like things
    spent in a great potlatch, this Texas barbecue
      of Asia, Africa, and all the Americas,
And the professional military behind him, thinking
    to use him as they thought to use Hitler
    without losing control of their business of war,
But the mania, the ravening eagle of America
    as Lawrence saw him "bird of men that are masters,
    lifting the rabbit-blood of the myriads up into   ."
Into something terrible, gone beyond bounds, or
As Blake saw America in figures of fire and blood raging,
    ...in what image? the ominous roar in the air,
the omnipotent wings, the all-American boy in the cockpit
    loosing his flow of napalm, below in the jungles
    "any life at all or sign of life" his target, drawing now
      not with crayons in his secret room
the burning of homes and the torture of mothers and fathers
    and children, their hair a-flame, screaming in agony, but
in the line of duty, for the might and enduring fame
    of Johnson, for the victory of American will over its
      victims,
    releasing his store of destruction over the enemy,
in terror and hatred of all communal things, of communion,
    of communism;
has raised from the private rooms of small-town bosses and
    business men,

> from the council chambers of the gangs that run the great cities,
>   swollen with the votes of millions,
> from the fearful hearts of good people in the suburbs turning
>   the savory meat over the charcoal burners and heaping their
>   barbecue plates with more than they can eat,
> from the closed meeting-rooms of regents of universities and
>   sessions of profiteers...

The poem doesn't hesitate to mention Johnson. Elsewhere it makes reference to Goldwater. It's a poem written in passion, not for the ages, but for its moment. This is precisely why it's a useful political poem. It may also be the reason it will last.

Student: Does the limited audience for poetry ever make you want to write in a different form?

Kinnell: I don't know that the audience for poetry is that limited. I suppose the best-selling novels published in the year the *Duino Elegies* were published have already disappeared, while the *Elegies* will last as long as human beings do. If I am tempted into another form—as I am sometimes—it's not because I seek a wider audience, but because of the possibility that another form can say something that poetry can't.

Student: Is there a great difference between a poem and a novel?

Kinnell: There are things which novels can do and say that poetry can't. It's mostly because of the novel's capacity to create a set of fully rounded characters, a set of people who can act upon each other. Poems can't do that easily. Ancient poems could, but only because they were actually novels in verse. The novel has taken narrative and naturalistic depiction of characters out of poetry. This is all to the good because it frees poetry to do something else, even to include some other things that normally belong to prose. In the traditional novel—say in a Henry James novel— there are delightful things all along the way, marvelous prosey descriptions of places and people and incidents. Aside from the other things the book does, these qualities make it worth reading. But when a novelist wants to say something that intensely matters to him, sometimes he will break in and interrupt his novel with what constitutes a kind of poem. Melville does it often. Even Henry James comes close to doing it. When Strether is talking to little Bilham in *The Ambassadors*, it's really James himself who says: "Live all you can. It doesn't so much matter what you do . . . so long as you have your life." These words could be the last lines of a poem. A poem can consist entirely of these moments of direct statement that most novels can manage only periodically.

Student: In your poem, "Path Among the Stones," do the stones represent poetry?

Kinnell: I notice that readers, especially those trained in universities, tend to look straight off for a symbolic interpretation. It's true that things in poems sometimes are symbolic, but not often in so direct and mechanical a way as this standing for that and that standing for this. Stones, for example. When stones come into a poem, they usually are actual stones. Part of poetry's usefulness in the world is that it pays some of our huge unpaid tribute to the things and creatures that share the earth with us. If stones were merely to stand for something else they wouldn't have much reality or inherent value. It's hard for a human to grasp the

reality of stones firmly enough to put them into a
poem, but some have come close, and it is poetry's
ambition. Here's a passage from a poem by Hayden
Carruth:

> The stone lies ample and smooth and warm and brown
> And at the same time blonde.
>
> I am stroking the stone with my fingers and my curved palm,
> And it is as soft as linen, and flows like the flax
> From the spindle.
>
> I would lie on the stone, reaching my arms down strongly
> To draw myself full to the stone and to fondle
> The flesh-gloss below.
>
> I would copulate with the stone until I became like stone . . .

That poem discovers that the aspect of the stone by
which we come closest to it is the last thing one expects
a stone to have—sexuality. This understanding, that
sexuality is at the very root of all things, even inorganic
things, also pervades this great and strange poem by
Abbie Huston Evans, "The Mineral Collection":

> I always knew the Ural Mountains glowed
> And burned inside with emeralds and gold,
> Copper in clefts, and platinum in rifts
> Like tamped-in tinfoil; now my eyes have seen
> Splinters from that great beam that braces Asia.
> Here in the dark, awake, I see again
> Rock out of Mexico, Siam, Peru,
> Thrace, Arizona, and the Isle of Malta;
> Rock out of Chile burning fiercely, furred
> With copper-blue like a kingfisher's feather:
> Rock out of Greece, imperishable blue,
> Cool blue of the Argives, lined with green of the sea;
> Delicate rock of India lightly dyed
> With milky azure, peach, and apricot;

Rock out of Maine, the ice-like tourmaline
In shattered spars, pencils of frigid rose
And chill black-green, of waters most dilute:
All these the bright credentials of dark workings,
Compulsions, interminglings, strangest love,
Knittings and couplings know but to the atom.

The thought of those bright fragments
    wrenched from darkness—
Of cinnebar, and slabs of malachite,
And crusts of amethyst—dazzles me still,
And raises me on my elbow in the dark.
Recalling topaz split and opal fractured
I tingle—great is life retired in stone!
Great is that obstinate impulsion launched
Against the opposition of the dust,
Whereof are we: we, and the red-cup moss,
The blowing tree, the boulder, and the fly
In amber under water; quick and slow
Braided in one, one indeterminate life
Riddling the dust. Show me one mote inert!

I don't know of a poem in the language which more truly accords to stones their own existence. It's a spectacular work and, like many spectacular works, almost completely unknown.

Student: Did you mean to say that there isn't any symbolism in poetry?

Kinnell: In poetry things often take on a certain "shimmering" quality. It's nothing that can be spelled out, it's something you feel. It happens all the time in Whitman. Whitman loved the world, probably as much as anybody who ever wrote. He loved its things, and its creatures, the whole scene of this world, so much. Nobody else has written long rapturous poems consisting of nothing but descriptions of things and people. Whitman himself was extremely quiet. When he did speak he was clear, precise, frank, direct. But what everyone noticed about him was that he listened well. He'd ride up and down Broadway talking with the omnibus drivers, or spend days and days on the East River ferryboats, up in the pilot house talking with the pilots. Everyone liked to talk with him. He could enter many lives. When you read his poems, the great passages, you find the things in them are never merely symbolic, they never just stand for something else. Yet Whitman opens himself and lets these things enter him. When he writes of them, he writes also of himself, with these things as his medium. They become his words. All his feelings for existence, for himself, for his own place, come out in what he says about them. So they take on a strange life, a vibrancy, that is *almost* symbolic. He rescues these things from death and lets them live in his poems, and, in turn, they save him from incoherence and silence. This happens in the greatest poems. It has something to do with what is called symbolism but it is not the same.

Student: I remember your poem on Robert Frost. Is it because Frost talked so much, as you said about him, and didn't listen, that he missed being another Whitman?

Kinnell: Of course, Robert Frost did love to talk, perhaps more as he got older. On the other hand, he spent a lot of time in solitude. I don't think the fact he was a talker prevented him from being receptive or from knowing silence. He wasn't the same kind of person as Whitman. He was fascinated by the speech of New Englanders, and by the lives they led and the things around their farms and so on. But he didn't devote his life to gathering it all in, the way Whitman did, to absorbing his own time and giving it back in poetry. So his poems are of a different character, of a more individualized, crusty, less flowing, character than Whitman's. In his best poems, Frost comes out with mysterious utterances that surprise even him. There is a lot of control and deliberate technique in most of his poems, but this doesn't stop him from making sudden frightening probes into the unsayable. "Out, Out . . ." and "The Vanishing Red" are poems where that happens.

Student: Are there any contemporaries who have the capacity to listen that way, in their poetry?

Kinnell: In the early poems of James Dickey—especially some of his animal poems—you can see a real capacity to enter sympathetically into another creature's life more or less in the terms I was talking about earlier. Dickey of course has a rich language, which helps. So do John Logan, W. S. Merwin, Allen Ginsberg, Tom McGrath. The music of their verse helps them to flow outward, to flow into things and creatures.

VIII

An Interview
Based on Conversations with
Don Bredes and David Brooks

Sheffield, Vermont, December 1975

Interviewer: Do you mind it that "The Bear" is the one poem of yours that people are likely to have heard of? Do you ever get tired of hearing compliments about that one poem?

Kinnell: Years ago when I met Norman Mailer I told him how much I liked *The Naked and the Dead*. He said "Thanks"—but there was a weary look in his eye. Someone told me that when John F. Kennedy met Mailer he praised *Deer Park*—probably Mailer's worst book—and Mailer was so impressed he was Kennedy's devoted admirer ever after. But then, I'm not John Kennedy—which probably explains away the point of the story. As for myself, I may get a little tired of the same compliment but—what shall I say?—I'm not truly exhausted.

Interviewer: You must be asked to read "The Bear" often—do you enjoy reading it?

Kinnell: It's a little hard for me to read it. People in the audience know the poem, so I think I should do something more with it, read it better, or something. Once in Ann Arbor, as soon as I announced the title of the poem a rustle went through the auditorium. I felt I could have paused a few moments, nodded, then gone on to the next poem, and no one would have noticed. When the poem was new, I'd often observe that at the place where the hunter eats the turd, people would look at each other apparently with disgust. These days the most squeamish dutifully sit through it.

Interviewer: Why do you think that poem of yours in particular is so popular?

Kinnell: I don't know. It's easy to grasp, because of its narrative. At the same time there's something raw or uninterpreted about it, and therefore you have to work at it, give something of yourself, if you are to get anything out of it. In that sense, it's a hard poem. But maybe if you like it at all you like it better than poems that require less of you.

Interviewer: You've talked about readings. I know you give many of them. What exactly do you try to do when you read?

Kinnell: I think the thing one tries to do is to articulate the poem as definitely as possible—delineate it with your voice and make it stay in the air of the auditorium long enough for the audience to take it in almost as well as they could if they were reading it from a book. I suppose the best metaphor would be that it's like skywriting. But the main thing is concentration—to be in the poem while saying it, rather than to "perform" it.

Interviewer: I notice you often recite from memory, without a book. Is that something you've practiced?

Kinnell: It just happened. It comes from giving a lot of readings. But I seem to know my new poems by heart too, as soon as they're written. I find the other thing surprising, that there are poets who can't remember their own poems. Many stand there with head bowed as though reading from a text written by someone else. James Wright reads from a book, but that isn't because he can't remember his poems, it's because he remembers all the discarded versions too. In the past, all poets knew their poems. If you couldn't say a poem by heart, it meant it hadn't entered your heart. I suspect some use a book because they don't like to look at the audience. But I think it helps to look at the audience. When circumstances are right the great mystery of poetry seems to unfold right there: you speak the poem to the audience, they listen and draw it in, and a peculiar closeness takes place, as if everyone in the room were living through some extremely private yet totally shared emotion. Afterward, of course, you may realize that for most of those who came it was just an evening's entertainment, and perhaps not too entertaining at that.

Interviewer: Do you think you've improved as a reader?

Kinnell: I'm not so nervous as I used to be. I'm sure this allows me to be more outgoing. Sometimes, recently, I've felt a terrific rapport with an audience—two or three times I've felt I was disappearing right into the words—"effusing my flesh in eddies." On the other hand, it has also happened recently that I've read very badly. Incidentally I must be the only person who's fallen asleep at his own reading—I arrived at a reading exhausted and in the course of it I propped my elbows on the podium, put my head in my hands, and actually fell asleep. It was just a few seconds. I woke up almost at once and carried on quite refreshed. I never learned if the audience had thought I was in a poetic swoon, or what.

The other day I listened to the tape of a reading I did this winter in a studio. It was one of the worst readings I've heard. The emotional words turn into quavering sighs and the sentences die out instead of end. That same day while looking for an empty take-up reel, I ran across a tape of a reading I had done at the Ninety-second Street "Y" in 1958. I believe it was about the fourth or fifth reading I had ever given. I listened to the tape, and I loved it. That person reading paid incredible attention to the meaning of all the words, he articulated each word completely, he even had a rather pleasant accent that seems to have gotten lost somewhere along the way, and the voice came down firmly at the end of the sentences, with a Yankee decisiveness, the way Richard Wilbur's does. It was a cool reading—no emoting, no quavering, just the poems straight. If I'd realized then how good I was, I would never have changed.

Interviewer: Do you ever get sick of reading?

Kinnell: Yes, sometimes. It's happened a few times that the whole thing has been a nightmare. I'm at a college where I've visited a number of classes during the day. There's been a cocktail party at which I drank in hopes of making the evening easier. At the dinner afterward a perfectly pleasant man—though with some little thing about him that irritates me, bad breath, or hair combed over a bald skull, or something trivial—asks me a perfectly pleasant question.

"What part of Vermont do you live in?" Suddenly I can't grasp that he's only trying to be pleasant. Out in

Wyoming or wherever we are it suddenly seems peculiarly absurd for someone to want to know what part of Vermont I live in.

"The northeastern part," I said glumly, knowing that's not the end of it.

"Is that near Burlington?"

"No, it's on the other side of the state."

"What's the name of your town?"

"Sheffield."

"What's it near?" It really isn't near anything so I tell him it's between Wheelock and Glover. "Is Glover near Bennington?" he asks. I now pour a whiskey down my throat. I see his hair pasted over his sweaty scalp, and I have a terrible desire to be somewhere far from here. The dinner goes on—"Isn't Putney somewhere near Sheffield?" I hear him saying. It becomes hard to extract a reply out of me. The others become uneasy and so their questions, too, grow rather pointless. Finally I drop into silence. Eventually they begin to converse among themselves, and seem actually to have a rather lively conversation. When it is time to read I am depressed. My dinner companions don't abandon their sullen guest, but for reasons of duty or curiosity or politeness or revenge—my sick spirit wonders which—they occupy the first row. There is a certain look a face in the audience takes on when it is daydreaming about something else—a sidewise, downcast look. I see many such looks as I drone on. At the reception afterward I wander around a bit and leave early. In the morning I know the time has come to stop these readings and go home. I also know that at 10 A.M. a certain Professor Alembick from Ag Tech will pick me up for the five hour drive to my next reading—during which he will not fail to explore with me the geography of Sheffield, Vermont. Once arrived I will visit the creative writing class, where they are spending the semester learning how to write sonnets, a section of freshman English, where I will be held up before the gaping faces like some item dragged in from the woods, and a course in contemporary poetry, where they will have now got up to Trumbull Stickney. Then I will drink my way through the cocktail party and try to gather up my spirits for the dinner that will now lie directly ahead . . . I'm going on about this. In fact things like this haven't happened too often, and not for a long time.

Interviewer: You spoke of the good audience at Ann Arbor. Do you find the audiences at the "Ag Techs," the community colleges, and so on, especially in remote places, able to listen to your poetry, which is fairly complicated?

Kinnell: Well, they need more practice. Listening to poetry isn't easy for anyone. At a poetry reading, unless you listen really well and stay with the poem, you don't get anything out of it at all. At a gallery you can look at a painting, turn away, talk, look again. I've seen people walk into a concert, immediately fall asleep, and at the end arise apparently quite satisfied, and even shout a "bravo!" or two. Which is reasonable enough, since while they were sleeping the music was flowing through their brains. At a reading, if you aren't following the poem, all you get is the drone. If a listener really hears one poem, hears it from beginning to end, and gets only scraps of the rest, it seems to me that's sufficient. For myself, the more interesting the poetry and the more suggestive its images, often it happens I start dreaming off in some direction of my own during the reading. Listening to poetry is hard; and harder when you haven't had practice. There are still places in the world where people find it natural and easy to listen—Iran is such a place, so apparently is Russia—but not here.

Interviewer: How do you like the way the Russian poets read their poems?

Kinnell: I like Joseph Brodsky's readings. He chants the poems; sometimes he comes very close to singing them. Like Dylan Thomas, he has both a natural understanding of the music of poetry and the voice to express it. By comparison, Yevtushenko and Voznesensky appear to me self-consciously theatrical. I don't like the self-assertion that's involved in the stage whispers, the shouts, the studied gestures, the strutting around. The dramatic style is an attempt to manipulate me, and I resist. I think that at a reading the voice should become so much at one with the poem it almost isn't noticed.

Interviewer: Thousands turn out to hear poetry readings in the Soviet Union. How do you feel poets are regarded in the United States? Do they have the status and respect they seem to have in other countries?

Kinnell: I haven't lived enough in other countries to be sure. When I lived in France, I often felt the French think of poetry as an extinct art. They not only don't have poetry readings, they don't have a word for them. Maybe things have changed and *le poetry reading* now exists. At the same time I'd sometimes encounter some unlikely person in France—a businessman for instance—who might know poetry very well, even know the young poets, and care for poetry a great deal.

It depends on the character of the people—their traditions. Even though the Russian middle classes are technocrats, like ours, they still seem to connect with the traditional past, where poetry was born. The fact that the Soviet government may send its nonconforming poets to Siberia, or forbid them to publish, is often put forward as a virtue, even if a very nasty one, evidence that the Russians take poetry seriously. During the Vietnam war there were probably those in the Justice Department and the Pentagon who would have liked to have thrown Denise Levertov or Henry Braun or Robert Bly into jail, but mostly our government is indifferent. That isn't so bad after all—at least it allows one to write, and to write what one wants—no small blessing, as the world goes. Yet for all our complaints it happens that the United States is probably the only country in the world where it's possible to live by one's poetry. This is mostly because the American university has decided to patronize the poets—by giving them teaching jobs, hiring them not for their academic credentials but for their poetry, and by sponsoring poetry readings. And of course the universities wouldn't do this were there not a strong interest in poetry among both students and professors. A poet with even a modest reputation can make his living from readings—provided he's willing to spend half the year on the road. Nothing comparable to our poetry-reading circuits exists anywhere else in the world, as far as I know.

But I've noticed an odd thing at the readings: even when the readings are well publicized in the community, there are seldom many adults present, seldom the equivalent of that French businessman. It's as though poetry were the exclusive domain of the young. In many countries poets have been asked to perform what is regarded as serious adult work—Neruda, Saint-John

Perse, Octavio Paz ... the list is long. But this has not happened here, except thirty or forty years ago when Archibald MacLeish was Librarian of Congress. Of course an American poet might well refuse a diplomatic post, but he can be sure he will never be asked. Our government assumes a poet is not quite a full adult—that he's a little too dreamy and bewildered for common work. It's a rather sweet view of the poet, possibly even flattering. Much as in the old days the eunuchs were put into the service of ladies, so in our day the poets are hired to serve and pamper the young.

Interviewer: You once said translation of poetry should be absolutely literal. Do you still think so?

Kinnell: I think straightforward, literal translations often convey more of the original than do poetic versions—at least those willing to alter the meaning in order to capture the "spirit" or reproduce the form. Robert Lowell's *Imitations* set, I think, a rather bad example. He uses literal versions of some of the world's greatest poems as if they were first drafts of poems he himself then finishes—changing them where he likes. If you change a poem you should be certain your changes improve it. But it isn't easy to improve on those great originals. Lowell is a marvelous poet, which is why I single him out, and yet his emendations usually diminish the original. What he does in full awareness that he is not translating strictly speaking, others practice thinking that they do translate. I could cite many examples, but there's no point without going into detail. The puzzling thing about translations is that even the alterations for the worse seem to be made for trivial reasons. Long ago I read an article about translating poetry—I've forgotten who wrote it—in which the author tells how he felt obliged to change "weasel" to "fox" in his English version, I think on the ground that weasels aren't as well known as foxes, or don't have the right associations, or for some other reason. The phrase, "the curious weasel," of course became "the curious fox." But anyone who lives in the country knows that the weasel is intensely curious and will pop its head out to see who's there when you walk by its den; he will also know that the fox isn't a bit curious. Another problem comes when translators want to reproduce the rhyme and meter of the original. Then the meaning *must* be changed. It isn't a matter of choice any longer but a consequence of the nature of language. Language does not allow the translation both to rhyme and to be accurate. When you write a poem, the words come to you as whole things, undivided into sound and meaning. When translating, the sound and meaning are necessarily two things. The translator is required to express a certain meaning, and he is also required to produce a certain sound. Sooner or later—usually sooner—to obtain the sound he must compromise the meaning. The cost in terms of this poem he loves is huge. The metaphors, the images, the specific understandings are slightly warped all for the sake of showing us—as if we needed to see it again— another example—one that is necessarily clumsy since it's imposed on a preexisting meaning that can be warped only so far—of the sestina or sonnet or rhymed couplet or whatever.

Interviewer: What do you think of poetry workshops? I know you've taught a number of them. Can one teach poetry?

Kinnell: No, one can't. Poetry consists of inner experience, the things of the world, and language, and of course none of these can be taught. Other arts involve communicable technique. Poetry doesn't. Its technique can't be separated from individual poems. To master someone's "technique" would be like taking on another identity. What someone who teaches a workshop mainly does is recognize the passages that are alive and true and show these to the author. Young poets are terrific at criticizing poems by others, but often in their own poems they can't tell the sublime from the junk. In that respect they're just like older poets. It would be better if poems were like pots, which slump and collapse when they aren't made right.

The best thing about a workshop is that it gives the students a place to meet each other and talk with each other. In European countries there have been atheneums and writers' cafes where young writers could come and listen and talk and perhaps show their work. In the United States up until recently writers have lived in extreme isolation. Take Frederick Goddard Tuckerman and Emily Dickinson, two of the three most talented American poets of their time. They were not far apart in age, they lived in neighboring towns—they even looked alike—but as far as I know they not only never met but never heard of each other. I don't think either of them ever met Emerson or Thoreau, though all four lived in the same state. Whitman met Thoreau twice I think. He met Poe only once, while trying to collect on a printing bill. The eccentric and original quality of the best writing of that time is probably related to the solitariness of the poets' lives, but so are some of its less desirable qualities. The poetry workshop has a lot wrong with it, but it's easy to see what need it was invented to fill.

A workshop is useful only if the people in it encourage each other. Then an excitement can come over the group. Everyone writes much more. One after the other they begin to write well. When it's over, there are perhaps no more poets than there were before—those who go on to do something doubtless would have gone on anyway—and one might say, therefore, that it has been a waste, a mere amusement. I don't agree. I think the exhilaration of speaking, as if magically, from the very center of one's being, is itself a blessing, and worth doing, even if only in one's adolescence.

Not that workshops can't also be quite unpleasant, especially when there are one or two super self-assertive, paranoid persons in the group, who hold everyone else's work in contempt, won't listen, and snarl and bite when cornered. Or sometimes you find the opposite: totally passive students who accept every suggestion that's made. "I'd throw all of that poem away except the third line in the fifth stanza," someone might say. "Oh, OK," the author cheerfully replies and would do it too, if someone who hadn't been listening didn't break in just then to suggest eliminating that very line. "Oh, OK," the author says just as cheerfully.

Most of the people in workshops are at a point where they aren't entirely sure of what they want to do in their writing. The real danger from a workshop, therefore, is that they may try to write to please the teacher, or with an ear cocked to the imagined reaction of the group. Also, the graduate workshops, the ones that lead to the MFA degree, seem to be breeding grounds of the careerism one sees in the poetry world today.

Interviewer: What about the experience of teaching a workshop, as far as your own poetry goes? Is it helpful in any way?

Kinnell: I've always known that teaching doesn't help. Recently I've begun to understand that it can actually be harmful. Tennis professionals say that spending all day teaching tennis ruins their game. In poetry, too, if you teach too much, there is a penalty. You encourage your students, you watch them improve, you praise them, you cherish their successes. In the end you begin to live in a world where all standards have been unconsciously adjusted slightly downward. Perhaps, too, it's that when teaching you lose sight of the main thing. You are so concentrated on helping students perfect their lines and images that you forget that poetry is a matter of vision and understanding, even awkwardly expressed, if need be; just as the tennis teacher concentrates on smooth strokes and may forget all about winning. But I do think that when you find a powerful talent among students, it's tremendously good for you. It's like translating, an opening of yourself to the influence of a new force.

Interviewer: I know you've never been a member of a workshop yourself. But have you had an equivalent experience, have you been influenced by teachers or your peers, have you shown your work and received criticism?

Kinnell: I was influenced very much by Charles Bell. And in the early sixties I lived in the same building in New York as Denise Levertov. We would show each other our poems. From her remarks I learned a lot about line breaks, economy, other technical matters I hadn't understood. I've had good advice from a number of others—most consistently from John Logan, Robert Bly, and Robert Mezey. Once I showed *The Book of Nightmares* in manuscript to the workshop I taught in Iowa, and they gave me many good suggestions.

Interviewer: I understand you're making an anthology of English and American poetry from Chaucer to now.

I suppose you wouldn't undertake a project like this unless you felt your anthology could be different. Have you found poets who are overlooked by other anthologies? Who would some of them be?

Kinnell: I'm just looking for good poems. It turns out that many of the poems I like best are not famous. I've included a lot of Smart's "Jubilate Agno," for instance, a poem of which you almost never see anything more than the fragment about the cat. I've put in a lot of Clare, who seems to me as good as any nineteenth-century English poet except Keats, and also a lot of Tuckerman. In the twentieth century there is a huge number of overlooked poets, far more than I can possibly put in the book—Edwin Muir, Laura Riding, Ruthven Todd, John Hall Wheelock, Abbie Huston Evans, Edith Sitwell. . . . Recently I ran across a fine poem by a poet I'd never even heard of—Alice Corbin. It's called "One City Only" and it goes like this:

One city only, of all I have lived in,
And one house of that city, belong to me . . .
I remember the mellow light of afternoon
Slanting across the brick buildings on the waterfront,
And small boats at rest in the near-by harbor,
And I know the tidal smell, and the smell of mud,
Uncovering the oyster flats, and the brown bare toes of small
    negroes
With the mud oozing between them;
And the little figures leaping from log to log,
And the white children playing among them—
I remember how I played among them.

And I remember the recessed windows of the gloomy halls
In the darkness of decaying grandeur,
The feel of cool linen in the cavernous bed,
And the window curtain swaying gently
In the night air;

All the half-hushed noises of the street
In the southern town,
And the thrill of life—
Like a hand in the dark
With its felt, indeterminate meaning:
I remember that I knew there the stirring of passion,
Fear, and the knowledge of sin,
Tragedy, laughter, death . . .

And I remember too, on a dead Sunday afternoon
In the twilight,
When there was no one else in the house,
My self suddenly separated itself
And left me alone,
So that the world lay about me, lifeless.
I could not touch it, or feel it, or see it:
Yet I was there.
The sensation lingers:
Only the most vital threads
Hold me at all to living . . .

Yet I only live truly when I think of that house:
Only enter then into being.
One city only of all have I lived in,
And one house of that city, belong to me.

What if Eliot or Frost, or other Olympian figures, had
been willing to speak of decisive moments of their lives
as directly? The poem affects me as much as many
famous poems—as much as most passages in the *Cantos*,
for instance. Do I exaggerate? Well, perhaps, but not
very much. The point is that even in the recent past
there have been many extremely talented poets—already
neglected or forgotten—who wrote a few extraordinary
poems.

Interviewer: Did rejections by magazines bother you
when you were young?

Kinnell: Yes. I hated any editor who rejected my poems. Now I don't take it personally, and I don't mind it—I'm actually grateful to editors who keep me from publishing a rotten poem.

Interviewer: Are there any responses to your poetry that particularly give you pleasure?

Kinnell: Yes—when someone, someone I know, or even more a stranger, tells me how much a poem has meant to him or her. Or when a letter arrives from a place I've never been. I find such letters are peculiarly affecting. If poetry were to need a proof of its reality, they would be it. I might also mention the royalty check—that curious distillation into money of the desire of people to own the books! I find the money that comes to me this way is like a present, totally unrelated to whatever labors earned it, and ought to be spent in a special way.

Interviewer: You've mentioned tennis. What is it about tennis that appeals to you?

Kinnell: If you really concentrate in tennis, mind, body, spirit, all become one thing—in this it's like poetry—a tremendously happy activity. But it's also the opposite of poetry, because it's an entirely escapist activity. I like it for both reasons. When the world is too much with you, you just put on your white vanishing-clothes and enter that court laid out in pure, Euclidean lines—and live for a few hours with increased life, like a wild creature.

It's an especially beautiful game and has appealed to poets. At one time or another in their lives Ezra Pound, Hart Crane, John Berryman, Randall Jarrell, all were devoted players. Theodore Roethke was not only an excellent player, but for a number of years he coached tennis. I'm just a grade B player. The best poet-players I know are Stanley Kunitz, who is nearly seventy, and David St. John and Ross Talarico, who are about thirty. Robert Frost liked very much to play, they say, but he hated to lose. In fact he would get so upset and grumpy when he lost that those who looked out for him arranged that no one could play him who did not agree beforehand to dump the match.

Interviewer: Do you have any advice for young poets?

Kinnell: No. They don't follow it anyway. That's the first bit of advice, don't follow advice. Oh, you know, platitudes, all the things mothers say: Don't waste time, (unless it's pleasurable to waste it), take care of your health, or at least its useful component, vitality. If vitality isn't everything, it's close to it. It's the reason children survive their childhoods. Artistic expression is most likely just surplus vitality. Vitality is constitutional but probably with effort can be ruined.

Interviewer: What about the "careerism" you spoke of?

Kinnell: I'd say—as distinct from what mothers might say—don't be too ambitious in that way. Forget about trivial ambitions—a reading here, a publication there—and have great ambitions in your writing. Yes, I really do have some advice—a piece of it, anyway, that's very practical: let there be a decent interval between being a student of writing and being a teacher of writing, a little space when you are simply a writer. Fear, not want, drives young writers into university teaching.

Interviewer: Here you are, an established poet a year away from being fifty. I suppose it would be an indication of how poets are treated in this country, if you could say whether the circumstances of your life are more or less as you might wish them, whether your life is arranged in such a way that you have what you need in order to write.

Kinnell: A good question. Hard to answer. In this respect my life changes from year to year. I seem to work harder at earning a living than I ever have, mostly because I need more money now than I used to. I don't mind any of the ways by which I earn a living. In fact I mostly like them. It's only that I'm rapidly becoming a writer who has no time to write. Time is the only necessary necessity. The hours after the children are asleep and before one goes to sleep oneself will do for some kinds of writing, but not for poems. I produce most and write best when I have no schedule at all, when I'm able to wander where whim carries me—both physically, through a city or a countryside, and mentally, in reading, talking, scribbling, thinking, whatever. Poems don't come to me often when solicited. More usually it's when I turn my back on them, and become absorbed in something that is not a poem—a thing, a creature, a moment, a face, a fantasy, a memory—that an understanding happens between me and that other, an understanding that brings with it its own words. Then I don't feel I'm making up the poem; rather my pen has to race to keep up with words that seem to be given. I complain about time. One can have a lot of time and yet feel one has very little. A person who wants an inner life needs what you might call "open" time—time that hasn't already been filled before one enters it with minor concerns, little duties. The more conscientious a person is, the more easily small things force themselves into the consciousness. Precisely because they are so small one knows one can easily take care of them. I keep finding in my pockets old lists of errands that in hindsight are incredibly trivial. It's the fact that the items are crossed off that's so pathetic—the fact that I actually worried about these tasks and actually did them. Tillie Olson has written an essay on the penalties of postponing serious work for the sake of things of this kind. It's a fine essay. She advocates going straight for the real work and to hell with everything else. And she's right. The creative drive withers away otherwise. On the other hand, she mentions how Rilke refused to go to his daughter's wedding for fear that he would thereby miss writing the poem that might come to him that day were he to remain in his study. Rilke may be the greatest poet of the century—I happen to think that he is—but sometimes when I read one of his poems I feel it's exactly the poem a man would write while staying away from his daughter's wedding—very spiritual so as to transfigure what in lesser spirits might be taken for callousness. It's true, and it's not true, what Auden says:

Time that is intolerant
Of the brave and innocent
And indifferent in a week
To a beautiful physique,

Worships language and forgives
Everyone by whom it lives . . .

It's easier for writers if they don't have children to raise, dishes to wash, or, as in my case, don't have mouths to feed, tuitions to pay, bank loans to repay. Or if they have plush jobs at a university. Or if they have an independent income. Or are married to someone who does. My circumstances are such that I live most of my life rather busily in the midst of the daily and the ordinary. This probably won't change very much, and so I want to learn better how to make use of the time there is. Turning a little time into a lot of energy probably is a simple act one can learn—like changing a substance from a solid to a gaseous state.

But whatever my poetry will be, from now on it will no doubt come out of this involvement in the ordinary. That's why I'm glad that not all the books that mean most to me were written by the angelic ones, the Rilkes and the Shelleys. Many are by writers who worked at earning a living far harder than I do, and at far less pleasant jobs. Anyway, here I am, almost fifty, struggling a little as you can see, in circumstances a little adverse, but on the whole hopeful. The angels can do almost everything surpassingly well, but one thing they can't do, they can't write out of adversity. This is a master we have that they have not.

IX

An Interview with Ken McCullough

Columbia, South Carolina, February 8, 1976

McCullough: Do you think the poet, the beginning poet, that is, ought to master the short poem, the haiku moment, before he attempts anything grander?

Kinnell: Well, I doubt if it's helpful. But then I doubt if it's helpful to follow *any* prescription that's supposed to be good for you. Probably it's not in the nature of the vocation to follow rules, at least those laid down by others. The hardest thing is to learn to go one's own way even if that way seems foolish to others. What if Allen Ginsberg had devoted himself to the haiku moment instead of writing "Howl"?

McCullough: You seem to disbelieve the idea that "you must learn the rules in order to break them." Do you also disbelieve that it is a waste of time for a poet to write poems in imitation of others? I don't see how you can avoid doing this.

Kinnell: I agree with you. And it's not a waste of time, it's one of the ways a poet learns. But I think it's a mistake to imitate someone's work deliberately, as a discipline—unless you can't help it, unless the model is an ultimate one, so that to write *is* to imitate. If one were to imitate, say, first Creeley, then Whitman, then Hopkins, then Jeffers, as a series of exercises, as a way of "practicing" poetry, I think it would disturb one's relationship with language. It would tend to give you facility—mastery over words—whereas what you want is to be the servant of words. Probably the only way to "practice" poetry is to write it.

McCullough: Should a beginning poet read his contemporaries, then go back to the masters?

Kinnell: I doubt if it's absolutely necessary to read one's contemporaries, but it *is* necessary to read the masters. If one has a profound connection with older poetry, no matter of what time or what place, like parental love it can only help to give one strength and identity.

McCullough: In the sequences, "Avenue C" and "The Last River," you seem to be trying to update the American landscape in the Whitman fashion. Is it possible to do it anymore? It seems impossible to have Walt Whitman's sense of the consciousness of the continent when the quality of our lives becomes more and more franchised every day.

Kinnell: It wasn't really my intention in those poems to follow Whitman in the way you mean, even though it may look like it. And I agree that it's not possible to speak of America the way Whitman did. He spoke *for* the country, as it was and also as he dreamed it, which is what gave his voice its peculiar authority and amplitude, what you could call its sense of destiny. The difference is that we know this dream will not come true. In this we're more like Hart Crane than like Whitman. Whenever Crane tries to speak in Whitman's bardic voice, he sounds strained and sentimental. *The Bridge* is devoted to celebrating the New World and yet its two greatest sections, "The Tunnel" and "The River," evoke only its outcasts. Like Crane, we write against history. Much of Whitman's poetry is devoted to celebrating ordinary sights and sounds and in this respect, the "Avenue C" poem probably does follow Whitman. But in my poem, time and progress appear as enemies, as they never do in Whitman.

McCullough: Ralph Mills said, "Like Roethke or Gary Snyder, Kinnell is attracted to the non-human world . . . as the basic context of man's living." Do you agree with this statement?

Kinnell: Well, yes, I do. The nonhuman *is* the "basic context" of human existence. Some let it come into their poetry more than others. When in the presence of wind, or the night sky, or the sea, or less spectacular instances of the nonhuman—including its revelation through the human—we are reminded both of the kinship and the separation between ourselves and what is beyond us. If there is one kind of moment from which poetry springs, I would say it's this one. Do you know Anne Sexton's poem on the night sky? It expresses a death wish and yet I think it is strangely life-giving—it expresses what you might call the *happy* hunger to die.

> The town does not exist
> except where one black-haired tree slips
> up like a drowned woman into the hot sky.
> The town is silent. The night boils with eleven stars.
> Oh starry starry night! This is how
> I want to die.
>
> It moves. They are all alive.
> Even the moon bulges in its orange irons

to push children, like a god, from its eye.
The old unseen serpent swallows up the stars.
Oh starry starry night! This is how
I want to die:

into that rushing beast of the night,
sucked up by that great dragon, to split
from my life with no flag,
no belly,
no cry.

So many of the great poems begin similarly—a feeling of strangeness and then of terrible kinship.

McCullough: Many people criticize *The Book of Nightmares* as too fatalistic. I see you resigning yourself to death, but there is still the great fear of the darkness which is so ever-present in some of the earlier poems. Whitman seems to have it down in the final section of "Out of the Cradle." Do you think you will ever come to grips with death in as positive a way as this?

Kinnell: It would be nice if I could. Whitman lived all his life in the double thought of death, both fearing death and desiring it. He began saying farewell to life while relatively young. As he grew older he was able to transfigure both the fear and the desire into a willingness to die and an even purer wish to live. In "The Last Invocation" he says,

Let me glide noiselessly forth;
With the key of softness unlock the locks—with a whisper,
Set ope the doors, O Soul!

Tenderly! be not impatient!
(Strong is your hold O mortal flesh!
Strong is your hold O love!)

I don't know that it's ever been said better, or that it can be.

McCullough: Do you ever find that your poems become self-fulfilling prophecies? Doesn't it bother you that the tail end of "Under the Maud Moon" in a sense is an admission of defeat or a commitment to tragedy? And in such statements as "Even this haunted room/all its materials photographed with tragedy." Tragedy is uplifting and exhilarating, but must it be self-immolation?

Kinnell: Well, at the end of "Under the Maud Moon," what I *meant* to convey was the hope that when my daughter comes upon hard hours in her life—as everyone does, I don't imagine for her any special miseries—she will open this book for what help it may be. At least it will tell her how much her father loved her. No, I don't take it as an admission of defeat. As for the "haunted room," I was thinking of one of the rooms in my house that people say is haunted. The walls of haunted rooms are supposed to hold the sorrows of their former inhabitants like photographic negatives. If we could know that everything in existence knows fear, even the ghosts, we ourselves would perhaps feel less afraid.

McCullough: Do you feel that dwelling on the dark side of the moon generally leads to disaster? It seems that, as Roethke found, each time you dive into the primordial slime, each time you go deeper, each time it's that much harder to come back up. Some do not make it back. The Orpheus myth. The poem, you say, is the "earthward gesture" of the skydiver. It is so tempting not to open your chute, isn't it? Must there be this risk involved in writing poetry for you personally?

Kinnell: Orpheus loves Eurydice, and therefore had to see her in the flesh. If any don't make it back for a similar reason, that's all right. For myself—and to take up the other metaphor—I am not tempted not to open the chute. When I was twenty, I used to think about suicide and a few times since then I have wanted to die. Not any longer. When I think there will come a time when I won't experience this world any more, particularly when I think one day I will leave my children forever, I can hardly bear it. One of Rilke's *Sonnets to Orpheus* tells us to "keep ahead of all parting." I guess I'm not doing that very well, and there is a sense in which I don't even want to.

X

An Interview with Jack Crocker

Lubbock, Texas, November 2, 1976

Crocker: I know you've said that you distrust discussions of poetry that are technical—

Kinnell: I *think* I distrust them. Perhaps I like them without knowing it.

Crocker: In your early poetry you started out with rhyme. Was that because of your schools, your teachers, or was it just the thing to do?

Kinnell: Well, of course, most of the poetry that I'd read, of the past, used meter and rhyme; so did most of the poetry that was being written at that time. In school and college little attention was given to writers who had broken with that formal tradition. Whitman hardly came into the curriculum at all.

Crocker: In your poem "For William Carlos Williams," at least in that particular setting, you indicate that even at that time he was not appreciated. He was politely received and the professor with the bow tie and wearing tweeds got up and scampered out. Do you remember whether you had discovered Williams at that time, or were you just generally indicting the academic community?

Kinnell: I hadn't really discovered Williams then. I had read him a bit but not very much. The moment I heard him, though, I felt close to him. The audience—it was at the Breadloaf School of English—seemed to me particularly unresponsive. Being a typically arrogant young man, I thought I was the only one there who understood him. Of course, in retrospect, I can imagine that many others also must have been moved by that evening, for it was marvelous reading. In any case, I sent the poem to Williams and got a note in reply, something to the effect that we're all swimmers against the tide. About ten years later, when I had got to know Williams, I mentioned this poem to him. To my surprise he remembered having received it. He said, "You know, I had thought it was such a good reading, until I received your poem."

Crocker: Had you already turned from formal structures then or was it after that you began to write in more open forms?

Kinnell: Well, I wrote quite a lot of free verse in college, in part I think because I found rhymes quite hard to work out. I was probably mostly just following the prevailing practices when I turned to rhyme and meter. By the time I heard Williams, I was writing mostly in formal verse and continued to do so for some time.

Crocker: It's interesting that you say at that time writing in rhyme was more difficult for you. Later, I think in the essay, "The Poetics of the Physical World," you make the statement that rhymed poetry is easier to write.

Kinnell: Rhymed verse is hard mainly because of the difficulty in making it all come out reasonably natural and idiomatic. And also because you have to spend huge amounts of time wracking your brain for the rhymes. Unfortunately, I always had felt it was beneath the dignity of the calling to use a rhyming dictionary. Sometimes I would spend hours and hours looking for a single rhyme, mumbling out all the possible rhyming sounds, alphabetically, in all their permutations, until I hit one that was actually a word. As you know, there are many words in English for which there are only one or two rhymes, and many with no rhymes at all— "sixths," for instance, which we can hardly pronounce, let alone rhyme. The poem has to confine itself to meanings that one of the available rhyme words can accommodate. It's here that rhyming poetry is "easier" than free verse. Seeing the possible rhyme words taking shape out there ahead of you, you aim for them. So the rhymes lead you forward and actively aid the composition of the poem. In free verse you have no such guide. You have nowhere to go except where the inner drive of the poem takes you.

Crocker: I remember when I was reading "To Christ Our Lord"—I responded to the content and I was also aware it had a rhyme scheme. Then I noticed something. I forgot about the content of the poem and said, "I've got to check this." I had noticed that in the next to the last line of each stanza, the penultimate syllable of the last word picks up the rhyme of the first line, and I noticed it in the first stanza. I said to myself, "He wouldn't do that all the way through!" But I checked and you did. At that point does it become a game?

Kinnell: Well, in a way, the moment you use a single rhyme, it all becomes a game. The game is not so much to accomplish the rhyme scheme itself as to see if you can produce within the elaborate form a graceful and serious poem. It's what in the Renaissance they called *sprezzatura*. But I think the effort that goes into these formal complications distracts you from things that matter more. I like "To Christ Our Lord" but I think it might have come out more interesting if it had not been rhymed. As it is, it's perhaps a little predictable. But I was so grateful whenever I managed the rhyme that I gladly overlooked a little predictability.

Crocker: Yet as reader the fact that I was involved with the form in no way canceled the value of the poem. I think my response was just as valid, you know, whether it had been free verse or formal.

Kinnell: Well, I don't think it's the formal qualities in themselves that make one feel a poem is just a *tour de force*. It's when the poem is at the mercy of the form.

Crocker: You have done quite a bit of translation, Villon and others. Does that have an influence on your own poetry?

Kinnell: Yes. When you translate you get about as close to a poem in another language as it's possible to get. It was Plato, wasn't it, who disapproved of acting as a profession because actors sometimes have to imitate people of base character. He knew that getting inside another person—as translators do, no less than actors—

changes you. After you translate, your own writing is never quite the same.

Crocker: I would like to talk some about the theme of death in your work. In the earlier poetry, a poem say like "Freedom, New Hampshire," there is, I feel, a kind of belligerence, that is both rebellious and regretful, in working out the problem of accepting death. In that poem you are dealing to a great extent with what you were to handle in *The Book of Nightmares*, and although there is still fear and the refusal to let go, as in "The Hen Flower," it seems by the end of *The Book of Nightmares*, there is a different attitude.

Kinnell: Our feelings about death change enormously, since time and circumstance are constantly putting us in a new position with respect to it. It's not easy for me to say how my own feelings about it have changed. But in that poem, "Freedom, New Hampshire," the unwillingness of the acceptance is mostly due to the fact that it's an elegy for my brother, who died when he was thirty-two. You can't "accept" someone else's death, least of all that of someone who died young.

Crocker: In the first section of *The Book of Nightmares*, "Under the Maud Moon," you are describing the birth process and you make a statement that at the moment of birth "it is all over," when your daughter is coming from under the hill and out into being—are you indicating in that the possibility perhaps of a preexistence, or a fetal consciousness? What is "all over"?

Kinnell: For the fetus, at the ninth month, its mode of life changes rather profoundly, that's all. There is surely a fetal consciousness. One can almost imagine it.

We grasp something of what the womb life might be like by listening to the recordings made of whales' singing.

Crocker: In "The Path Among the Stones" you develop a terrific image of nothingness, with the wafer stone that skips ten times across the water creating circles that obliterate themselves. That zero after the numeral one in the tenth section of *The Book of Nightmares*, is that it?

Kinnell: I don't take at face value the doctrines that suggest some further individual life for a person. The most difficult thing for the human being is the knowledge that he will die; everything else can be dealt with, or could be, were it not for that knowledge. And so we develop, one after another, some manner of accounting for death, or of turning it aside, or of making it more tolerable. All the theories of personal immortality or personal resurrection or personal reincarnation very likely are results of wishful thinking.

Crocker: Is eternity then only possible in the sense that we die back into the universe or, as seems to be the case in "The Path Among the Stones," that we dissolve into the stone? At the end of that poem it seems you arrive at the merging of life-death, physical world-spiritual world. Is this a kind of Emersonian correspondence?

Kinnell: Yes, I guess there's a streak of Transcendentalism in all this. While eternity is only our word for some condition we don't understand, yet in the greatest moments of our lives, we do grasp that there's an element beyond our reach, from which we came, and into which we will dissolve, which is the mother and father of all the life of the planet, to use terms which may apply better than we think. Our happiness in this life—our capacity to sense this element—makes us able, when the time comes, to die willingly, to return to it without bitterness or the feeling of having been betrayed.

Crocker: Since this is November second [1976] and America is electing a president today, I would like to get into politics a little. Some of your poems are political. I'm thinking of "The Avenue Bearing the Initial of Christ into the New World" and "The Last River" in particular. The old ideal which America has historically represented seems to be referred to along with the corruption of the human and political process and the Vietnam war. Is America beyond the promise of a "new world" or was America ever possible in those terms?

Kinnell: I don't know if America has become very different in this regard, but hopefully our understanding is clearer. The term "the American Dream," of course, gives it all away. At least part of what goes for political wisdom in this country is simply the disappointment we all come to feel after being raised—at least prior to Vietnam—in such a narrow and self-congratulatory idealism.

Crocker: Taking it one step further, what about Western civilization in general? In "The Dead Shall Be Raised Incorruptible," there is a rather savage view of Christian man. Is the whole Christian process based on a false assumption?

Kinnell: "Christian man" is the term I used in that poem for "technological man." Technology is the latest of the methods we use to overcome the fear of death. Probably the sense of dominion it gives us allows us to suppress the knowledge of our own mortality. It's not a very healthy frame of mind and it doesn't make me cheerful about the future.

XI

An Interview with Margaret Edwards

Sheffield, Vermont, August 27, 1976

Edwards: Do you have trouble writing about other people, especially people you love, who might feel hurt by what you say?

Kinnell: I've felt some qualms, but not in the way fiction writers might. Since in a novel one has to present a whole, believable person, one tends to lift a lot of actual detail from the lives of people one knows best. This is OK—except when a recently divorced author tries to get revenge. But since verse isn't well suited to depicting people in any detailed way, this isn't a problem in most poetry. Shakespeare's sonnets tell us almost nothing about the person addressed, not even if it's a man or woman. In my own poetry there probably is less autobiography than there seems to be. It's often imagined that writers take actual persons and protect them with fictional names, but I seem to do the reverse—give actual names to more or less fictionalized characters. I think those I'm closest to know this and are not too upset.

Edwards: Do you think a person has to be crazy or unbalanced in some way to be a writer?

Kinnell: I guess there has to be something wrong with you. If everything were satisfactory, you might sing, as do the dolphins, but you certainly wouldn't sweat out long novels or involved poems. But crazy? No, not really. The people who are called crazy because they see through existence, those for whom there are no verities in this world, are surely the most gifted of us all, as far as poetry goes, but they are usually unable to write and perfect a poem. Rilke's very elevated sensibility was grounded in the capacity for uninspired, plodding, hard work. Hard work concedes the reality of this world. Discipline, determination, and ambition—illusions for the people I'm calling crazy—are probably requirements for someone who wants to be a writer.

Then there's what you might call "real" craziness. As readers, we can't surrender to a work we feel has been written by someone controlled by paranoid suspicions and sick fantasies. The poems we love are those in which we believe we find the truest and most encompassing understandings. The poets we admire are the ones whose responses to experience we feel are reliable. In this sense the best poets are the sanest.

Edwards: What about the poems which manage to foist their dementia onto the reader?

Kinnell: Well, yes, many obsessed poems draw us in by their single-minded intensity. But even the maddest of these, the medieval romances and love poems, try to reach a whole understanding, even if like *Tristan and Iseult* they exhibit only the destructive side of their subject, the passion that leads to death. Among the handful of poets I like most are Christopher Smart and John Clare. Both wrote their finest poems while supposedly mad. But in these poems you find an incredibly intense clarity and selflessness, divine madness and divine sanity both at once. Here's a passage from "Jubilate Agno" that might give an idea:

> For the flowers are great blessings.
> For the Lord made a Nosegay in the meadow with his disciples and preached upon the lily.
> For the angels of God took it out of his hand and carried it to the Height.
> For a man cannot have publick spirit, who is void of private benevolence.
> For there is no Height in which there are not flowers.
> For flowers have great virtues for all the senses.
> For the flower glorifies God and the root parries the adversary.
> For the flowers have their angels even the words of God's Creation.
> For the warp and woof of flowers are worked by perpetual moving spirits.
> For flowers are good both for the living and the dead.
> For there is a language of flowers.
> For there is a sound reasoning upon all flowers.
> For elegant phrases are nothing but flowers.
> For flowers are peculiarly the poetry of Christ.
> For flowers are medicinal.
> For flowers are musical in ocular harmony.
> For the right names of flowers are yet in heaven.
> God make gardeners better nomenclators.

Everyone knows that human existence is incomplete. Among those who are especially troubled by this are those who turn to writing. Writing is a way of trying to understand the incompleteness and, if not to heal it, at least to get beyond whatever is merely baffling and oppressive about it.

Edwards: I take it you don't think writing makes a person more unbalanced, yet how do you account for the fate of Crane, Berryman, Kees, Jarrell, Plath, Sexton, and others?

Kinnell: A. Alvarez puts forward the theory that writing intensely about one's own pain increases the pain. I don't think it does. I can't demonstrate this. It's an article of faith. I think poetry brings us more, not less, life. When it happens that a poet commits suicide I find myself looking in the poetry for the flaws.

Edwards: Is this also true of Sylvia Plath, whose poetry seems to get better the closer she comes to death?

Kinnell: It's complicated. I'm not really sure. Often an element in the suicide of writers seems to be loss of creative power, a loss of interest—frequently brought on through too much drink, or giving up drink, or relapsing back into drink, I don't know which is the most deadly! In Plath's case there's none of this. In her last years she is more energetic, interested, and clear-sighted than ever. A terrible intensity comes over her, kindled on the emptiness, that makes it appear her art required her to destroy herself. Yet I think it's mistaken to see her as a doomed goddess. Her husband had left her. She was alone with her children. It was cold. Things were going badly. One of her reactions was to sulk, if one can judge by the poems. Suicide, or attempted suicide, is the ultimate form of sulking. She thinks her own woes are the only ones and ceases to understand that other people suffer, often more grievously than she. Other people don't exist in these later poems except to the degree they cause or reflect her pain. I am not taken by her use of Nazi concentration camps as a source of metaphors for her own situation. Also, it often seems she doesn't want to understand her misery so much as to intensify and perfect it. Each poem becomes a quest for the image that will lacerate her most. So her poetry is marked by self-absorption, self-pity, and melodrama. I know this is a harsh judgment. But you see, I respond very much to her poems, and it is these elements in myself, as much as in Plath, that I'm trying to be clear about. All criticism is self-criticism. What anyone says about anyone else is only provisionally true. In fact, when it comes down to it, we know very little about the real forces, the actual emotions, that drive a person to commit suicide. And I'm ready to concede that I could be wrong about the connection between a life and an art. There remains the rather romantic possibility that a destructive, despairing life can produce a poetry that gives us only health.

Edwards: Which poets of your generation do you think are writing well these days?

Kinnell: A number of poets who've been writing beautifully for years I'm glad to say still are. I'd give you a list, but they'd be poets you've known a long time. I'm struck by a few poets of my generation who've blossomed more recently. Doubtless they themselves feel it wasn't so recent. I've felt Philip Levine used to hold something back, as if for fear poetry would betray him into tenderness. In his recent poems, it has done exactly that. Donald Hall has stopped writing those poems crafted according to the best critical principles and has started writing what you might call simply *poetry*— saying in its own music what matters most to him. Their new poems are marvelous. Hayden Carruth's *Paragraphs* are among the most exciting new poems I've seen. Carruth has been unfashionable and unread for far too long. Another splendid "late-bloomer" is Gerald Stern.

Edwards: That's an interesting—and rather simple—description of poetry: "Saying in its own music what matters most." Do you, as a poet, think critical theory about poetry in general is excessively complicated?

Kinnell: I suppose some equally simple statement about poetry has been made many times, by those who react against a convention-ridden poetry, by Wordsworth and Coleridge, for example, or by Pound and Eliot. But perhaps it's too often taken for granted that the problem lies with a faulty poetic theory, and so can be solved by a correct theory. I suspect it isn't a matter of theory but a personal, psychological, question: whether one can get past the censors in one's mind and say what really matters without shame or exhibitionism. It seems to me the four poets I mentioned were quite lucid with regard to the evasions that the poetic conventions of the day encouraged their predecessors to practice, yet they in turn fell into evasions of their own—Coleridge less than the others.

Edwards: Sometimes I suspect you of thinking that form is itself an evasion.

Kinnell: I'd like to agree—but I'm really not quite that bad. Anyway it's a long story—one that someday I may write. All I'd say now is that I don't think the term "form" should be applied only to such things as stanzas of uniform size, rhyme schemes, metrical patterns, and so on—elements which may be regarded as external trappings. I think form properly speaking also has to do with the inner shape of the poem. Some of the most "formal" poems are rather formless in this sense: they change subject, lose the thread of their arguments, and lack the suspense and sense of culmination that come from the pursuit of one goal.

Edwards: This is one of those peculiar, but human, questions: Do you indulge any old habits, quirks, or rituals in the process of writing?

Kinnell: Not really. I prefer to write with a pen. And I must have a Smith-Corona portable circa 1935 to copy the poems with. I own three of these machines. They look a bit the way my poems feel to me. Also, they creak along at about the speed of thought—my thought, I mean.

Edwards: Do you feel unhappy when you haven't written for a long time?

Kinnell: Yes, a little, sometimes. In the last few years especially, when I've written less than earlier. It's irrational. It should be no great worry if it should happen that one stops writing. In fact it should be rather bracing to go on to something new. But it's not that way. Writing is the one trade you can't give up. The history of literature is filled with poets who've gone on all their lives desperately, doggedly, turning out verse to maintain the dream they are poets. Wouldn't it have been better if Wordsworth had taken up innkeeping or journalism? Rimbaud was the only one able to give it up, and that was probably because he hadn't been at it long. The difficulty is that by comparison other occupations are less interesting. To give up writing would be to close the door on one's deepest experiences. It is no consolation to think back on work already done. On the contrary, the *Moby Dick* in one's past is only a brutal reminder of how inattentive, shallow, and faithless one has become. The fear that comes from not writing is the fear of inner deterioration. They say that by tying a dead hen around its neck you can train a dog not to chase hens. There's nothing you can do about an aging poet—even if you tie around him a copy of the late poems of Wordsworth.

Edwards: Your speaking of hens reminds me of something I'd like to discuss. I teach *The Book of Nightmares* and there are certain questions students often bring up. I'd like to ask you a few of them. First, "The Hen Flower." What is your fascination with hens? Why devote a whole section of the poem to this one creature?

Kinnell: My family had a henhouse out behind our house until the Pawtucket city fathers zoned it away. I was very young then, perhaps six or seven, and I remember the chickens mostly through a few images. One is of my sisters plucking them. I don't suppose they ever stuffed a pillow with these feathers, or that we ever laid our heads on the feathers of a hen we were at that moment digesting—but it seemed a possibility. And I can see my father hatcheting the hens' heads off on the old grey log he'd set on end for the purpose, and then letting the headless creatures run about. I don't think any of the times I've killed hens myself are more vivid than these memories. Though not very personable, hens have an unusual psychic dimension, due, I like to think, to the suppression of their capacity to fly. When you hold their heads under their wings they slump into a strange coma. You might think they think it is the night, except that they do the same thing if you turn them on their backs and stroke their throats. They'll lie there for several minutes, apparently in a trance. Maybe the throat is their Achilles' heel, emotionally speaking, and they've fainted from too much. But they also fall out if you face them toward infinity—if you draw a straight line in the earth and hold them down with their beaks touching it. There are doubtless other mysteries in the hen.

Edwards: What about that "tiny crucifix" at the center of the earth? It has made some students assume you are Catholic.

Kinnell: I wanted to retain the Christian terminology, but to alter its reference. I wasn't trying to say that the cross of Jesus lives at the very center of existence. I was supposing that a body that presses down on the earth creates under itself a "shaft of darkness" that gets smaller and smaller as it approaches the center of the earth, until at the bottom it makes a formalized shape—which here happens, due to the form of the outstretched body, to be a cross.

Edwards: Could you say something about the "Dear Stranger" section? I find it hard to figure out. Explain the Juniata. Who lives there? And who is Virginia?

Kinnell: The Juniata is a river that flows through southern Pennsylvania. It's Virginia who lives near it. I guess that isn't clear. Virginia is an actual person I've had a long correspondence with. She is a mystic, a seer. She is one of those born without the protective filtering device that allows the rest of us to see this humanized, familiar world as if it were all there is. She sees past the world and lives in the cosmos. In an old issue of *Poetry*—or perhaps it was *Time*—there's a review of Malcolm Cowley's book of poems, *The Blue Juniata*. The review says the region Cowley writes about belongs to the past, no longer exists. So I allude to the fact that Virginia found it amusing to have her own sense of nonexistence thus confirmed. ("You see," I told Mama, "we just *think* we're here.") In this case, the "I" is Virginia—that *is* confusing.

Edwards: Have you ever met her?

Kinnell: Only once. We had coffee together somewhere in Pennsylvania, I think in 1969. It wasn't a successful meeting. Mostly we warily circled those strange containers, each other's bodies. I think it's the opposite of what Plato thought. I think that if people know each other only mind to mind they hardly know each other at all. Later, it was again possible for us to write trusting letters and even to reestablish an intimacy, though we now knew it was in part illusory, being purely platonic.

Edwards: Students occasionally get confused as to who's speaking the various quoted lines in "The Dead Shall Be Raised Incorruptible." I'd like to have it spelled out, if you don't mind.

Kinnell: The person who says "Lieutenant! This corpse will not stop burning!" is just some soldier on some battlefield somewhere—presumably Vietnam, since death by burning characterized that war. The man with the broken neck is also a soldier, though in fact the lines came when I was thinking of victims of lynching in the American South. And it is the membranes, effigies, etc., the memories of itself left on the earth by the human race, which is imagined to have destroyed itself, who pray for earthly experience to continue no matter how painful or empty it has become. ("Do not let this last hour pass/Do not remove this last poison cup from our lips".) The line, "We shall not all sleep, but we shall be changed," is quoted from the Burial of the Dead.

Edwards: What about the man who addresses the Captain?

Kinnell: That's supposed to be a conversation during a hospital visit. The Captain comes to see his tailgunner who has been put in the mental ward. I copied down that speech nearly verbatim from what a man told me who'd been in the Korean war.

Edwards: Someone you knew?

Kinnell: No, it was a stranger. I was with James Wright and Robert Bly on a barnstorming tour of New York State colleges in the spring of 1966, giving poetry readings against the war, sometimes two or three in a day. After the final reading, at Cornell, the three of us went to an all-night diner in downtown Ithaca. We had spent a whole week talking about love and peace. The moment we walked into the diner a man with the peculiar clairvoyance of drunkards came weaving over to our table and said, "Want to fight?" James Wright, who has great presence and also a prodigious memory which can pluck the right phrase from any of a thousand movies, said, "We're not fighters, we're lovers." So the man sat down and told us his story. He had been the tailgunner in a plane assigned to fly over Seoul to protect the city from enemy aircraft. From time to time when he saw civilians in the streets he would fire a few bursts at them, sometimes wounding or killing them. After a number of such incidents, he was given a medical discharge. For the next fifteen years, evidently, he had remained unable to understand his behavior. As he talked, one moment he was boasting of the feeling of power the machine guns gave him as he fired at the scattering figures, and the next he was weeping with shame. So he had become the town drunk—or one of them. I wanted to get this schizophrenic quality into the poem.

Edwards: That section is followed immediately by "Little Sleep's Head Sprouting Hair in the Moonlight," a very sharp contrast.

Kinnell: Yes, well, it's a special time—those minutes—hours sometimes—we spend with little children in the middle of the night. I've always liked getting up and going to my children. I'm partly asleep myself—most of what we call personality, or individuality, we leave back there in our bed. The child, too, is half asleep. So we hold each other, creature and creature, clasping one another in the darkness. We probably have to know each other well by daylight for these cosmic hugs, almost devoid of personality, to be possible. It is good for the child that the hugs take place, for during them something "sets" inside that will make it possible to experience a similarly primal embrace later on, in adult life, with a lover. It's like happiness. Everyone uses the word, but it's obvious that many don't really experience it and never will, probably because they were not disposed that way as little children.

Edwards: Could I ask about "The Porcupine"? In what way is it an "ultra-Rilkean angel"?

Kinnell: I was thinking—as I seem to do often—of the Ninth Elegy, where Rilke tells how the angels are attracted by ordinary, earthly things. The porcupine eats anything with salt in it -generally things we've handled a lot, that the salt of our sweat has soaked into. So, like Rilke's angels, the porcupine loves axe handles, doors, chair arms, and so on. A porcupine once ate the insulation off all the wires in my pickup truck, for the road salt. But it's mostly wooden things they like. Once they actually ate their way through the cellar door of this house. If they had climbed the stairs into the house itself, they would have reduced the place to rubble, since it is splashed—floor, walls, and ceiling—with my sweat. As it happened they didn't get in, because they ate down the cellar stairs on the way up. Farmers regard them as pests, and kill them on sight.

Edwards: I would like to go back to what you said earlier: "It's the opposite of what Plato thought. I think that if people know each other only mind to mind they hardly know each other at all." Once you said something that struck me in its simplicity of truth—we were talking about friendship and you said, "The body makes love possible." Just that. It was only a sentence in a conversation, but I've never forgotten it.

Kinnell: I remember that conversation. It was last fall, when you were driving me to the train in Montpelier. We had been talking about something Jean-Paul Sartre had been quoted as saying, something obviously spoken out of his own experience—which surprised me, since for some reason I had always thought of him as "mental," a theoretician, one of those who are just brains carried around by a body. He was talking about how deeply one communicates in a relationship that combines friendship with sexual love. He spoke about how language itself comes from the deepest place, from sex, particularly when love is involved. Our conversation had gone on I think to my days of teaching a correspondence-school course. But after all this talk in which I explain and explain and often feel I get nowhere, I think I'll keep still and leave at least that one phrase, which in its simplicity *does* seem to have the ring of truth, unexplained and possibly still true.